LEADERSHIP IN THE TRENCHES

Proven Success Strategies for Middle-Managers to Thrive in a System They Didn't Create

Karen Hauschild

First published by Ultimate World Publishing 2022
Copyright © 2022 Karen Hauschild

ISBN

Paperback: 978-1-922372-69-7
Ebook: 978-1-922372-68-0

Karen Hauschild has asserted her rights under the Copyright, Designs and Patents Act 1988 to be identified as the author of this work. The information in this book is based on the author's experiences and opinions. The publisher specifically disclaims responsibility for any adverse consequences which may result from use of the information contained herein. Permission to use information has been sought by the author. Any breaches will be rectified in further editions of the book.

All rights reserved. No part of this publication may be reproduced, stored in or introduced into a retrieval system, or transmitted in any form, or by any means (electronic, mechanical, photocopying, recording or otherwise) without the prior written permission of the author. Any person who does any unauthorized act in relation to this publication may be liable to criminal prosecution and civil claims for damages. Enquiries should be made through the publisher.

Cover design: Ultimate World Publishing
Layout and typesetting: Ultimate World Publishing
Editor: Maddie Johnson
Cover photo copyright license: Yulia Moiseeva-Shutterstock.com

Ultimate World Publishing
Diamond Creek,
Victoria Australia 3089
www.writeabook.com.au

Testimonials

"*Leadership in the Trenches* is an insightful examination of the challenges faced by middle managers in the modern workplace. Karen's passion for equipping managers with the tools they need to succeed is woven throughout the book. If you could have a fairy god-mother in your organization, you would want her to bring you a copy of this book. This is a valuable resource for everyone's management toolbox!"

Mary C. Bergstrom, M.Ed.
Senior Director for Institutional Research and Data Management at Quincy University

"Reading *Leadership in the Trenches* is like sitting down over coffee with a fellow mid-level manager. Karen has lived it and she gets it. Often an unappreciated, overlooked position, Karen gives the detailed attention to the job of mid-level manager that it deserves and requires. This is a one-stop shop collection of resources for mid-level managers. Karen provides an indispensable tool for navigating the roller coaster of responsibilities that fall on the shoulders of mid-level managers. She provides real life examples with strategies, resolutions and solutions. I wish someone had given me this when I started in management."

Edie Cusack
Executive Director, R.E.A.C.H Program

"Karen Hauschild's book *Leadership In The Trenches* reads like a modern-day version of Homer's *Greek Odyssey*. It is an easy to digest collection of key points a mid-level manager must navigate in order to be effective; the Scylla of being alone in the role to the Charybdis of incongruent organizational policies.

The content isn't novel or new. Many books have been written on each of the topics Karen covers. The novelty is that it's written in key situations one will encounter and Karen opens that content for review using her own experiences. Think of it as an easy listening podcast- only in written form!

Each chapter has a list of to do's for the reader to take what has been presented and commit to a course of action. Beware! You will finish the chapters fairly quickly and then spend the real work of creating your action plan for change. It is a wasted opportunity to skip past the action planning and read the next chapter. If you find it uncomfortable, you should probably ask why.

Being a leader in the trenches is not for everyone. For those reading this book, you are reminded continually that others have faced the same challenges you face now or will face in the future and that you are not alone."

Mike Zeinstra
Deputy Director, Human Resources,
NC Dept. of Public Safety

Dedication

This book is dedicated to the greatest blessings of my life. To my husband, Tom. Thank you for always believing in and supporting me. Our two halves make a pretty great whole. And to our awesome children, Holly and Carson. You both are an inspiration and make us so proud. May you always lead well.

Contents

Testimonials	iii
Dedication	v
Introduction	1
Chapter 1: Only the Lonely	5
Chapter 2: Captain of the Ship	15
Chapter 3: The Middle Child	29
Chapter 4: Man in the Mirror	41
Chapter 5: A Matter of Taste	55
Chapter 6: Needle in a Haystack	73
Chapter 7: Do Not Pass GO	91
Chapter 8: I Didn't Volunteer for This	103
Chapter 9: I Did a Great Job, I Promise	111
Chapter 10: Multi…what?	123
Chapter 11: People Are Who They Are	135
Chapter 12: Pretend They're Naked	145
About the Author	151
Acknowledgements	155
Afterward	157
Offers	161
Testimonials	163
References	165

Introduction

Phil 2: 3-4 [3] Do nothing out of selfish ambition or vain conceit. Rather, in humility value others above yourselves, [4] not looking to your own interests but each of you to the interests of the others. – New International Version

Welcome to your middle management role. Or perhaps you've been in this position for a number of years. Either way, congratulations! Being a middle manager is a tough place to be in any organization. You have some authority but often not enough to affect the kind of change you desire or authority to make the decisions you would like to make. I have been a middle manager for many years now and understand your pain. This is why I've written this book. I have read many books and articles and attended many workshops about being a good leader throughout the last two decades. The one thing that many of these readings and experiences did not provide me with was practical, day-to-day items I could do to use what influence I did have. Many of these articles or workshops are directed towards leadership of executive teams, but I have not yet encountered one that speaks to the challenges middle managers face specifically. We really are in the trenches. We're in between two battle grounds: the people supervising us and the people we supervise. While a trench is designed for protection, I don't think organizations make middle management a safe place to be, per se. Without the tools and skills for success, your trench could fill with water, and you may find your boat sinking. It is your responsibility to ensure your team can swim. If you feel like you are barely keeping your head above the surface, or that you do not even know where to begin, buckle up for some great information for not only self-discovery, but also practical tools you can use to make your work life better.

Many of the books about leadership I have read were written by a founder — the person who created the company, brand, or consulting firm, for example. They may have never spent time in the middle, and I imagine that if they did, they did not stay there long. Nevertheless, these authors are leaders and business owners. They make the decisions and ultimately get the final say. They have established the rules for their organization — and rightfully so. It's their business and they have likely spent countless hours building and protecting it. I have learned a wealth of information and gotten tons of ideas about how to improve myself and my leadership skills, but there were not many I read that had me closing the book after the last page with something tangible to do with my team. To date, I have not read any books about being a TRUE middle manager. I have crafted my way in middle management because of the various successes and failures I've experienced while working in this role. Yes, the books I have read helped me avoid some calamities that I may not have otherwise seen coming, and for that I am thankful. They have also shaped my thinking about leadership and the massive responsibility it is to do it *well*. In my work-life experiences, I have found that many people aspire to a leadership position because of what is in it for them, instead of what they can do for others. They may get these defined middle management positions for the credentials alone, regardless of their wherewithal for success. They may stumble into the role or it may be thrust upon them. It may have been because they were selected by family or friends to lead a department, group, or organization, but far too few have invested any time in thinking about what it actually takes to be a good leader. They are passionate about their group, cause, product, or service but lack the skills to rally, organize, hire, or evaluate

Introduction

people in their daily work. Working under such a defined leader can be painful. You do not want to be one of these leaders.

Working in an organization with systems you didn't create and have limited or no influence over has its pros and cons. The good news is you have these systems to help you navigate the policies and procedures of your organization. You have these systems, like your Human Resources department, to help you navigate tricky or tenuous personnel situations. If you're lucky, you have a next line supervisor who has your back and who hopefully has worked there longer than you and has their own tales of woe and success to guide and support you in navigating the company's culture. The bad news is that often no one above you or even beside you explains how to use these systems. It's on-the-job training at its finest. Many of the mistakes I have made as a middle manager have simply been a result of my own ignorance to a process, even when I thought I understood it. Or because the process changed, and the change was not communicated properly. The bad news is that sometimes these systems are old and antiquated, and no one can tell you why things are the way they are when you question their validity or lack of efficiency. I really hate hearing the classic phrases, "this is the way we've always done it" or "we don't do that." It kills me.

Competence leads to confidence. So does having the skills to successfully run your department from the middle. Most of the time you cannot control what's coming from above, and you (and your department) are left to pick up the pieces of a misplaced or misinformed decision or asked to implement a plan with little or no consultation about your resources. These directives are likely done by a well-meaning person seated one, two, or even three levels above you, but intentions do not translate well when you are not consulted. It is a constant tug of war, and you are stuck on the short end of the rope. So, since you likely cannot control or have a voice in what is happening above you, this book is filled with lessons learned and practical things you can do as a middle manager to control what you can.

As you might imagine, becoming a good leader is not a sprint but a marathon — a layering of lessons and people and projects, one of successes and failures. It is about making the best decision, not the most popular one. It is both exciting and exhausting at the same time. But at the end of each day, you must remember your 'Why,' and why you will return the following day to face the challenges in front of you.

It is about your people. What an awesome responsibility.

CHAPTER 1

Only the Lonely

"If one's different, one's bound to be lonely."
– Aldous Huxley

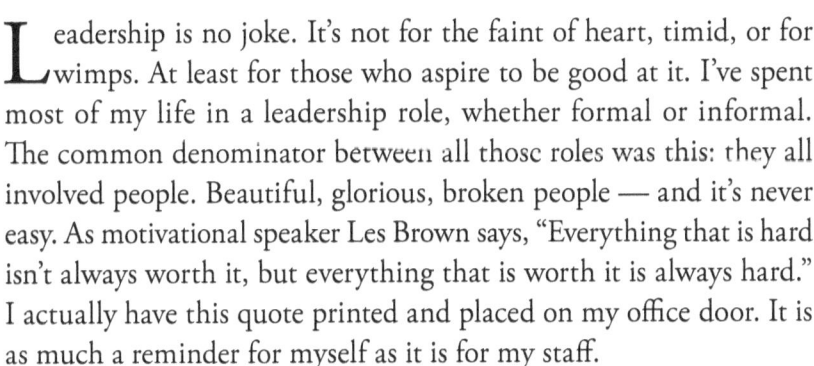

Leadership is no joke. It's not for the faint of heart, timid, or for wimps. At least for those who aspire to be good at it. I've spent most of my life in a leadership role, whether formal or informal. The common denominator between all those roles was this: they all involved people. Beautiful, glorious, broken people — and it's never easy. As motivational speaker Les Brown says, "Everything that is hard isn't always worth it, but everything that is worth it is always hard." I actually have this quote printed and placed on my office door. It is as much a reminder for myself as it is for my staff.

Leadership in any occupation can be lonely at times. You make decisions that impact you, your department, and your team. All of which impact their lives and the lives of your customers. This is no small task. Being a leader is often isolating because you cannot always speak to people in your department about the why behind your decisions. You also cannot speak about personnel or the rationale behind hiring decisions. You cannot explain 'the other side of the story' with employees. So, why, if it is so lonely, would someone want to be a leader in the first place? Why would anyone sign up for that? I think when you're not a leader, the role may seem glamorous and trouble-free. Yes, the defined leadership role may have a nicer office or a higher salary, but it also comes with more responsibilities. So, if you're questioning whether taking on this challenge is for you, then ask yourself, why not you?

Even if you're not the CEO or president of an organization, as a middle manager you can still influence the things you have control over. While the rules may be archaic or antiquated, there is often room for interpretation and creativity on the part of the leader to have an impact. If you understand the rules and work to develop your leadership skills, life for everyone under your influence can be better, which results in reduced personal stress and burnout and can impact the longevity of not only your own career, but also reduce your employees' attrition.

Developing soft skills such as communication, problem solving, teamwork, and emotional intelligence, among others, is crucial in understanding the people who work for you and being able to effectively lead your team.

Did you know that the largest source of stress for employees is their supervisor? And that the majority of people quit or are seeking new jobs because of their boss or a lack of appreciation? This is especially true in the realm of middle management. After all, if you're second or third in command, and you're hungry enough, you may choose to tough it out with a difficult boss in an effort to move up or prepare to move out. The question to ask yourself is, "Do you want to be the reason people leave your organization?"

This chapter will cover the importance of self-development. Leadership expert and author, John Maxwell, says everything rises and falls with leadership, and he's right. Over time I have tried to find a way for this not to be true, but as Maxwell says, "The hardest person to lead is the person in the mirror." What will people say about you as a leader when you're no longer there? (or behind your back to others?) What will your legacy be?

Only the Lonely

According to 2021 leadership statistics collected by Apollo Technical Engineered Talent Solutions, less than 5% of companies have implemented leadership development across all levels[1]. This is a terribly depressing statistic, and therefore it is crucial that you take the initiative to develop yourself.

In the summer of 2021, I participated in a livestream virtual Leadership Summit hosted by Ramsay Solutions. One of the first things Summit host, Dave Ramsay, said on day one was "leadership is lonely." It was such a relief to hear him say that. I have often thought this myself but was too afraid to say it out loud. I think many leaders may avoid admitting this because it can be perceived by others as a weakness, incompetence or lack of confidence.

So how do we overcome this feeling of loneliness? For many years I just sucked it up and figured it came with the job, so I either ignored it or pushed through it. However, in recent years I have found this isolation to limit my ability to be more creative in my problem solving and quite frankly, develop relationships with other like-minded leaders. Even if you have a great relationship with your next line supervisor, it is always good to talk with other leaders on the same level of the organizational chart to hear their perspective, get feedback in a safe environment, or help them troubleshoot something that is going on in their department or vice versa. Take the time to meet with these other leaders regularly. I would suggest at least once a month. Schedule it just like you would any other important meeting during your work week. Select the people you meet with wisely. As motivational speaker Jim Rohn says, "You're the average of the five people you spend the most time with." Not everyone is a great leader or aspires to be a great leader, so you want to meet with someone who is equally as hungry as you, if not more, to develop as a person and as a leader. With great support, a great relationship will blossom.

One of the struggles I have had over the years as a leader is understanding the real or perceived barriers of my role as 'the boss.' I have found that no matter how you slice it, at the end of the day, you're still the boss. There will always be a power dynamic in the relationships you have with the people you supervise. Therefore, having relationships with other leaders is so important because this power dynamic does not usually exist. I have learned that while I consider myself to be approachable and easy to talk to, not everyone perceives me this way. I have had staff members find the door frame to my office door a significant barrier to come in and talk to me, even though my door is open all of the time. I have had staff members tell me that because my stand-up desk does not face my office door, they do not feel comfortable coming in to talk to me. Maybe this is more about them than it is about me, but it did make me think when I got this feedback.

I have made it a personal goal to check in with each of my staff members at least once a week to see how they are doing and how I can help them. I pride myself on knowing a little bit about each person and about their families and lives outside the office. I remember a time when there seemed to be a lot of staff strife and stress. The water cooler chit-chat was palpable and staff members were becoming increasingly irritated by things they wouldn't ordinarily be bothered by otherwise. I realized that this may have been due in part to not communicating as much as I should, so I decided I needed to have a real heart-to-heart meeting with my staff. I felt particularly vulnerable during this meeting because it was important to me that I put myself out there, and when you do that there is always a chance it will not be well received. As I was addressing the questions and concerns at hand, one of my staff members said in front of the entire group, 'but I need this job.' I was stunned. I was stunned because I thought this person knew me better than that. After all, I felt like we had a pretty good relationship, but clearly not as good as I thought. I had no idea where this came from, and the comment did not particularly fit into the conversation. Nevertheless, I addressed the concern at the time and assured the entire team that no one would be losing their job. I went on further to explain that the system we worked in did not allow for immediate dismissal under most circumstances. After reflecting on this after the meeting was over, I realized that perception is reality. I also realized that no matter what I do, I will still be 'the boss.' I cannot change the layout of my office or the invisible door that fits within the frame. I can only work to continue to build relationships with the people I work with day in and day out to make the communication flow.

You must invest in your own personal and professional development. This takes time and intention. Almost everything I have learned about leadership has been from a book I purchased or a workshop oftentimes offered by my place of employment, both of which are low or no cost. However, the other most 'costly' lessons have been from my own painful mistakes. It is my hope that you learn from the wisdom of those experiences. Other methods for your own personal and professional development can occur through attending conferences, webinars and talking with colleagues in your professional organizations. With the abundance of resources at your fingertips through the internet, Google and YouTube, there is no lack of content with a quick click and keystroke. Attending conferences, both inside and outside your profession, is beneficial on multiple levels. It gets you out of your office and out of your head. You also get to talk to other professionals who may be facing some of the same challenges as you.

No Matter What I Do, I Cannot Seem to Make Everyone Happy

You're right. You cannot. Take it from someone who feels chronically responsible even for things I am not responsible for…like someone else's happiness or their response or reaction. You must let go of this expectation you have of yourself to make everyone happy. Instead, work to manage the expectations of others about your role. You can do this by communicating your expectations, values, and job duties to the people in your department and then remind them again and again in both formal and informal ways, like staff meetings or regularly scheduled one-on-one sessions, or through organic hallway or office conversations or in response to questions.

I'm Not Sure I Can Do This

Of course you can! The very fact that you are reading this book is a testimonial to your desire to grow as a leader. I have felt unsure of myself on countless occasions, but I just feel the fear and do it anyway. This can be any situation ranging from having a difficult conversation with someone to leading a full-day retreat. Your success lies in your preparation and your preparation lies in you carving out time to learn.

It Takes Too Much Time or Money

Yes, you are right. It does take time. However, you can spend the time investing in yourself and building your team by leading in the direction you want them to go, or you can spend time dragging them along, micromanaging, or worse yet, causing them to leave after you have invested time, money and company resources onboarding and training them. Yes, sometimes these activities cost money. However, it does not have to be your money. I have found very creative ways to stretch what little funds I do have access to by moving money from one item to another in my budget, inquiring about any extra funding through my next line supervisor, or looking to find grant funding either inside or outside my organization.

At the end of the day, you must decide that you are going lead, regardless of the circumstances. If you don't know what to do, do what you do know how to do and start from there. The world of work is ever- changing and you must remain nimble and employ new ideas.

STRATEGY TIME:

1. Set S.M.A.R.T. (Specific, Measurable, Attainable, Realistic, Timebound) goals related to investing in yourself. It could be reading a book a month on a leadership topic. It could be reading a daily leadership blog, listening to a daily podcast, or a two-minute video on a specific subject.
2. Attend workshops offered by your Human Resources department. As I mentioned earlier in this chapter, most businesses do not offer any leadership development program or training much less systemizing your understanding of the policies and procedures of the organization. This is often left up to you. Take advantage of what is offered by marking it on your calendar and making it a priority. If there is nothing available, look to outside resources such as inexpensive offerings through your professional organization or in the local community. Hopefully, there is a little bit of funding available through your departmental budget or from your next line supervisor so that you are not paying for your own professional development out of pocket.
3. Surround yourself with other 'on purpose' leaders. This could be someone in your organization who you aspire to emulate, or you'd like to have mentor you. If you decide to go the mentor route, be sure you both are clear on the expectations of that relationship.

"I have the worst and best, loneliest and most social, most appreciated and most thankless job in the company. And I do that job with pride and without complaint. Because that was what I signed up for." – Liam, character in The Motive *by Patrick Lencioni*

ACTION PLAN:

- In the next five days, I will:

_____

_____

_____

_____

_____

_____

- In the next 10 days, I will:

_____

_____

_____

_____

_____

_____

Only the Lonely

- In the next 30 days, I will:

_____

_____

_____

_____

_____

_____

_____

- The person/people I need to talk to about this are:

_____

_____

_____

_____

_____

_____

_____

CHAPTER 2

Captain of the Ship

"It's not hard to make decisions when you know what your values are." – Roy E. Disney

I have learned over the years if your actions and decisions aren't aligned with your values and an organization's mission, vision, and values, then you are positioning your ship to sink faster than the Titanic. As the defined leader, you are the captain. Your values ground your leadership philosophy and style. They inform the unwritten rules of the workplace. They establish your 'moral authority.' This is a term I learned from author and pastor Andy Stanley's Visioneering podcast several years ago[2]. There are unspoken expectations people have of their leaders based on a set of values. These values could be driven by faith beliefs or culture; but at the end of the day, I think they all fall

> Leaders with high moral authority always go first but think of themselves last.

into the qualities of your character. I like to think of it as leaders with high moral authority always go first but think of themselves last. This is in both tangible and intangible ways.

One of the supervisors I had in the late 1990's shared her values with our team at one of our first staff meetings as a new team, and I was really impressed. There is a certain level of trust that is established when someone in authority is vulnerable enough to share themselves publicly in this way. I decided that day I would do the same if I ever got the opportunity. So, I wrote down my values. I must admit it was much more challenging that I thought it would be. In those days, I was supervising college students and was much closer in age to them than I would be now. Each year I would communicate my values to them and share my expectations. When I formally moved into middle management and I was responsible for supervising adults, that changed for two reasons: I was no longer the defined group leader, and it was no longer my role where it would be appropriate to do this. While I still grounded my daily behavior in my values, I tucked my list neatly away until I recently dusted them off to revisit them.

As a middle manager, I don't think I've ever heard my next line supervisor tell me what their values were, much less the president or CEO of the organization. Of course, I made some assumptions about their values because we worked in the same place and believed in the company's mission and product, but I have never had one verbalize their values to me in a formal or systematic way.

The problem is that most people have never taken the time to identify their personal values, much less written them down. Being a leader that cannot articulate their values is problematic because it leaves your team wondering how you make decisions, and it makes the decisions you do have to make even harder. If your people do not know what you stand for, then they will not stand for you.

This chapter will discuss how your moral authority and personal values can impact your decision-making practices and help build trust with your team. Having moral authority lets your team know you are always going to do the right thing and make good decisions on their behalf because they know what you value. A leader must always go first and think of themselves last.

There is a difference between delegating a task because you need to and delegating a task because you do not want to do the task. This is one of the fastest ways to lose moral authority. It is similar to a parent saying, "Do as I say, not do as I do." This does not land well on a teenager and this type of attitude does not land well with someone you supervise either. While your team might not have expectations that you will help them with something, consider the increase in trust and your moral authority if you do something first. However, it is not a one and done activity. This attitude is something that must be consistently applied. You do not want this to be to the exclusion of the things are you are responsible for in your role; but anyone on your team should know that if they ask for help, you will give it and if you can anticipate places and times where you can help, you increase your moral authority. Consider times in your workweek or in a particularly busy season where you can intentionally step in to help. For example, when the phones are ringing off the hook, can you take some time to help answer the telephone? Or if someone calls in sick, can you help ease the burden on the rest of the team by stepping in somewhere? Sometimes doing things like this might prevent you from completing your To Do list for the day, but you will increase your moral authority.

As theologian, humanitarian, and Nobel Peace Prize recipient, Albert Schweitzer said, "Example is not the main thing in influencing others. It is the only thing."

If sacrifice is involved, the leader must go first. If money is requested, the leader must go first. If there is a company deadline, the leader must go first. If you are asking folks to share something about their lives, the leader must go first. As Schweitzer said, "There is surprising power in going first. Whether it's choosing music at home, or favoring a course of action at work, the first person to voice an opinion or take action becomes the point of reference for everyone else who comes after. Unless it is clearly a poor choice, people will tend to follow the lead of the first."

One of the organizations I worked for was facing a severe budget crisis and there was talk of layoffs and furloughs. Employees grew more and more anxious as the grapevine moved its way through the organization and folks were positioning themselves to avoid being cut and preparing for the worst. At a critical juncture, the president of the organization announced that he and other members of the senior leadership team would be taking short-term pay cuts in an effort to balance the budget and avoid furloughs. Granted, most of the members of the senior leadership team made a significantly higher salary than their lowest level employee and it likely did not put a significant strain on their personal finances, but they definitely gained points for their moral authority.

A more exaggerated example is the 1996 blizzard on Mount Everest. Reporter Jon Krakauer, who was a participant for this expedition, wrote a book about it entitled, *Into Thin Air*. There have been multiple documentaries and movies made that showcase the disaster. There were many catalysts, one preceding the other, that resulted in the tragic outcome. One of the key players was Rob Hall, owner and expedition leader for Adventure Consultants, who ultimately perished in the blizzard. There were many decisions he made that day, but two that negatively contributed to the fatal outcome the most were deciding to try to reach the summit past the turnaround time, which was 2:00 p.m., despite weather warnings.

"Close to 4:00 p.m., client Doug Hansen finally reached the summit with the assistance of Rob Hall, who remained behind to see his bid through. Shortly after, Hansen collapsed and Hall refused to leave him, setting the stage for a tragedy. Both were trapped on the South Summit by the storm," Krakauer wrote.[3] Clearly, Rob was committed to his clients and did not leave Hansen behind, which is what you would expect a good leader to do, but his own ambition and desire to secure a promised 'deliverable' had him make decisions that lead to both of their deaths.

Another fateful historic event that addresses moral authority is that of the April 1912 Titanic's sinking. It is a fantastic example of the captain's moral authority. Captain Edward Smith trusted the workmanship invested in the creation of his vessel and valued the technology of the day. He trusted it enough to the point of excluding feedback from his staff that there was an iceberg ahead. As a result of a decision that came too late, the ship hit said iceberg and approximately 1500 passengers perished. Who was last off the ship? Well, no one knows for sure. There are many disputing accounts of Captain Smith's final moments, but most accounts indicate that Captain Smith went down with the ship, or some variation thereof, and was painted a hero.[4] Certainly, had he jumped ship first or survived while so many others perished, it may have been considered a maritime crime at the time.

A more modern example is of the Italian cruise ship, Costa Concordia, whose captain, Francesco Scheittino, in 2012 ran his cruise liner into rocks, which resulted in 32 passenger deaths. Instead of staying onboard and ensuring the safety of his passengers and crew, the captain prematurely departed on a lifeboat to ensure his own personal safety. He was sentenced to 10 years in jail for manslaughter, and an additional five for causing the ship to wreck and one year for abandoning his passengers[5].

As I mentioned earlier, many leaders do not take the time to identify, much less articulate, their personal values. Years ago, I taught a course to freshman students wherein the students needed to earn a point value between 290-300 points to earn an A in the course. Most assignments were between 25 and 50 points each. I told the students at the beginning of the semester that we would be having an auction at the end of the semester, so when I returned their graded assignments, attached would also be play money in the amount of the points they earned. All college students understand the value of money, mostly because they usually don't have enough of it to make it through the weekend. So, if a student earned 23 out of 25 points on an assignment, attached to it when it was returned to the student would be 23 'dollars.' The most a student could earn in the semester was 300 of these 'dollars.'

On the last day of class, as promised, we had an auction. However, instead of auctioning physical items, we auctioned off lifestyle values (although I did spend time finding small trinket items that connected to those values). For example, for the value 'flexible free time,' a tangible item might have been a rubber band; 'access to culture' might have been a ticket stub or concert event flyer or poster; 'physical health' might have been an apple. I think you get the picture.

The students were always very excited for this event. In advance of the auction, I gave them a worksheet they could use to budget their money against the values noted on the worksheet and record what they actually spent on that item. As you can imagine, values such as a happy, intimate relationship, family, money, and job satisfaction were hot items, and some students spent all the money they earned that semester on them. These students were all in and very clear on what was most important to them — to the exclusion of all other available options. Other students divided their money among the items and in the heat of the moment, busted their budget to get what they wanted.

At the end of the auction, we spent time talking as a class about why they made the bids that they did and where the line in the sand was for them in winning the value. Some students got caught up in the moment and wanted to win something instead of walking away empty handed. Other students sacrificed other values for those that were most important to them. Sometimes, students pooled their money to help others win what was important to them.

As you think about your own personal values, take the time to dig deep. Most people would say that they value their friends and family. They likely would also value job satisfaction. Money is also somewhere on the list. Take a few moments now to brainstorm a list of your personal values. However, dig deeper than the obvious. What really drives your decisions? Here are some ideas to get you started: creating something new, impacting others positively, having reason, having compassion, having integrity, listening to others, freedom to work as you please, developing yourself, putting your faith in action… the list could go on and on and there are no right or wrong values. These are yours and they are personal.

Once you have your list, now prioritize them. Give them a score between one and five. One is low and five is high. Depending on how long your list is, you will have many that you have assigned a one, two, three, four or five. They all could be the same number. However, for the sake of the exercise, really think about the list. Clump like or similar values together. Can you cluster them? For example, you might cluster like values in larger value sets like PEOPLE, COLLEAGUES, THINGS, CREATIVITY, FAITH, SECURITY, or some of the larger clusters I mentioned earlier, like family or finances.

Once you have given each a numerical value and put them into value clusters, if appropriate, spend time now identifying the clusters where most of your five values have landed. These are the values that are the most important to you and from where your decisions will be influenced most. Ziad K. Abdelnour, Founder, President & CEO of Blackhawk Partners, Inc. and best-selling author, said, "A great leader has brains, vision, values and heart."

You may be thinking that you do not want to think about your values now. I submit to you that not knowing who you are and what you are about is like building a castle on quicksand. It may be scary to even think about them, much less share them with your team. However, being vulnerable with your staff will allow them to know you better and anticipate your response and reactions to things, which builds trust. Think about it this way, even if you never say a word, your values will emerge through your daily behavior and the decisions you make. Consider how much farther and faster you can go with your team if they don't have to guess.

There are unwritten rules of the workplace. Some of those include showing up to work on time, staying until the end of your shift or workday, speaking nicely to people, doing the work that is assigned to you, doing it well and completing it on time, or not talking behind others' backs. Of course, there could be many others one might add to the list depending on your industry, but these few listed here are universal to the world of work. When colleagues do not operate within these unwritten rules, others get irritated. These things seem like common sense, but as the father of one of my former supervisors used to say, "Common sense is only common if everybody knows it." Not everyone understands these unwritten rules and therefore they fall into the definition of what professional workplace behavior looks like. When these are violated, confusion, frustration and distrust unfold. Therefore, being a leader that leads by example and creates a workplace culture that operates under shared departmental values is so important. Over time and with consistent application, these values will become the unwritten rules of your workplace.

Developing a Leadership Philosophy

Do not rob your team of becoming a good leader. I recently heard on a radio show that the difference between robbery and a theft is the use of a weapon. When you rob your team of who you are, your weapons could be your silence, insecurities and doubts, or lack of knowledge and being OK not knowing. Getting to know who you are as a leader is as important as getting to know each member of your team. Developing a leadership philosophy is your next step.

A philosophy is a set of standards, values, ideas, and beliefs under which a leader operates. This is the passion and purpose behind your work. This is what drives you. This is what keeps the ship steady during turbulent times. This is what helps keep you focused. Actor and producer Tyler Perry says that "if a leader has no purpose, then you are like an expensive yacht with no rudder."

Whether or not you have ever articulated your leadership philosophy, you still have one. Leaders must take the time to develop and articulate their philosophy as a leader. This helps set you apart from your colleagues who are simply showing up on the job without purpose for their work.

Before you begin, you must consider the various leadership styles that are out there. The internet is loaded with articles and information about what each of these styles looks like in action, so I encourage you to take the time to research what each of these are. According to Indeed.com, here are the 10 most common leadership styles[6]:

Autocratic	Bureaucratic	Coach
Democratic	Laissez-Fair/Hands Off	Pacesetter
Servant	Transactional	Transformational
	Visionary	

Captain of the Ship

One of the two leadership styles I subscribe to that is not noted by Indeed.com is Situational Leadership. This theory was developed by Dr. Ken Blanchard and Dr. Paul Hersey and suggests that no leadership style is better than another. Instead, leaders use this adaptive style to meet the demands of the workplace when compared to the experience, skills, and workplace tasks for each employee. It also factors in the maturity of each employee and the leader's relationship with them. For example, new employees will need much more attention, guidance, and feedback than perhaps a staff member who has been in their role for many years. It is highly probable that you would give a seasoned employee more complex tasks or responsibility than a new staff member[7].

When I first learned about this model, I did not directly supervise anyone, so in some ways it was difficult for me to fully understand and embrace this practice. However, as I have matured in my own leadership, I have found this model to be very effective. I am sure you have had supervisors in your life who micro-managed you. This could have been due to an assumption you needed more support than you did because you were new or perhaps you started on the job with zero support and were left hanging. I'm not sure which is better.

Situational Leadership is often good to use in situations in which you have high turnover and you are constantly onboarding and training new people. This is particularly challenging because when you lose a staff member, you lose not only their knowledge and know-how, but you also lose their person-power. In some cases, there may be no one left to delegate tasks to except the already overworked, overburdened remaining staff and it may fall to your shoulders as the leader to pick up the slack and keep the ship afloat. When this happens, your role as leader often falls to the role of manager. It is about doing the tasks that run the organization, instead of leading the people that make the organization run. As I mentioned in the last chapter, everything rises and falls with leadership. The team suffers when you consistently have to manage more than you lead. Managing requires that you deal with putting out the fire each day. I say that sometimes it feels like chasing butterflies. You flit over here to deal with one issue and then you run over there to handle something else. Sometimes, you have to do this to make sure the processes and details are handled. You are focused on today and if you're lucky, maybe tomorrow or this week. However, leading requires you to be one step ahead so you can reduce the chances of a fire starting in the first place. You are charting the course weeks, months, or perhaps years in advance. Of course, there are times when what must be done, must be done. And if you are occasionally left to answering the telephone or sweeping floors, then you as the leader must do so. Your people will appreciate it. I also see this falling into a Servant Leadership practice, which is another style that I subscribe to. I tell my team all the time that they are there to serve our customers and I am there to serve them.

Nevertheless, regardless of your leadership style, and they all have their pros and cons in some way, you need to consider what works best for you for now and grow into the one you aspire to employ. With that, you must operate from your leadership philosophy.

To help you get started in your thinking, grab a piece of paper or sit down at a computer and complete the following prompts:
- My personal values are…
- What matters most to me as a leader is…
- I am a leader because…
- My current leadership style is…
    - Am I happy with it?
    - I need to change…
    - I would like to try or do…
- Leadership matters to me because…
- Think about the best and worst leader with or for whom you have ever worked…
    - What was your relationship with that person?
    - What behaviors did they exhibit that you liked? You didn't like?
- Good leadership looks like…
- As a leader, I can teach my team…
- I embrace the following leadership principles…

- As a leader in my organization, it is important to…
- My greatest accomplishments as a leader so far have been…
- The difference I want to make is…
- I develop myself professionally by…

STRATEGY TIME:

1. Take the time to identify and communicate your values. Write them down. Revisit them regularly. Update them as you get to know yourself.
2. Research different leadership styles, consider your values, and write a leadership philosophy.
3. Always onboard new people by being clear about what your office's values are and the expectations you have for their behavior.
4. Communicate that philosophy to your team.

ACTION PLAN:

- In the next five days, I will:

_____

_____

_____

_____

_____

_____

- In the next 10 days, I will:

_____

_____

_____

_____

_____

_____

Captain of the Ship

- In the next 30 days, I will:

_____

_____

_____

_____

_____

_____

_____

- The person/people I need to talk to about this are:

_____

_____

_____

_____

_____

_____

_____

CHAPTER 3

The Middle Child

"For decades, middle managers have been human routers: tracking project status, moving information across teams, and serving as intermediaries between junior employees and senior leaders." – Harvard Business Review

Being a middle manager is often like being the middle child. At times awkward. At times lonely. You have the ability to be independent but are not given complete freedom. You have a next-level supervisor to look up to and support you. You can lay low when the pressure is on the senior leadership. But you can also be the scapegoat. You have more responsibility but not necessarily any more authority. It is easy for decisions to be made by those above you that impact you without any consultation *with* you. You often feel

> You often feel as though there is a rope tied to both wrists: one to your next level management and the other to the people you lead.

as though there is a rope tied to both wrists: one to your next level management and the other to the people you lead. So why do it? As we discussed earlier, it is important to think about your motivation for leading. Are you leading for your own personal gain or are you leading to improve the lives of others? Where is your desire to lead? The answer to this question will make a difference as to whether you are perceived to be a boss or a leader.

As a middle manager you straddle an invisible line between the people above you and the people you lead. A key success strategy is understanding your organization's policies and procedures. You must make your department work and manage change with little or no authority within the larger organizational structure. This is challenging.

This chapter will provide an overview of the key elements every middle manager must consider and pay attention to in order to be successful in their role. The shocking truth is that most managers learn these things on the job instead of through formal training. In my own experience as a middle manager, most of my mistakes have been made because I did not have all the necessary information to make a better decision. This is not because I didn't ask questions or the information wasn't available. It was because I didn't ask *enough* questions or the rules for engagement changed and were not communicated. To be clear, not understanding the practices, policies and procedures, and possibly even organizational traditions and cultures, will cause you to make mistakes or slow down your decision-making processes. You always want to keep in mind your moral authority. When the rules change, how you navigate these changes puts your moral authority at risk.

It sure would be nice if we had a crystal ball so we could see into the future and understand the hearts and minds of those steering the ship above us. I have worked for numerous large and small-scale organizations and while some of the policies and procedures between them were very similar, others were very different.

One example is how a budget works. In one organization, when an employee resigned, their lapsed salary could be used for other purposes other than personnel. In another organization, those same funds were 'swept' by the budget office, and you had to request them back to use them, but they could only be used for staffing purposes. The challenge within the latter system is that while there was a form to complete and submit to the budget office, the approval process was very mysterious. It was mysterious because the personnel action you were proposing in the meantime had to be approved by a supervisor and a litany of others, including Human Resources. Sometimes those processes did not intersect in terms of timing because the paperwork was sitting on someone's desk for approval. The budget office would not approve the funds' use until Human Resources gave it the OK. It was so convoluted that I wrote the process down step-by-step and ran it by a colleague of mine who had been there much longer than me to make sure I understood it. My colleague told me that it looked correct but to be mindful that it may change without warning or communication. Sometimes these processes can be updated when a new person steps in a role and asks, 'why are we doing it this way?' I have always found it refreshing when someone asks this, because organizations get caught up in their ways and rely heavily on their policies, procedures and processes and once set, never go back to review if those same policies, procedures, and processes still make sense.

Now, back to my story about the swept funds process. Once I understood it, I was able to use it to my advantage as a leader. The people in my department were not highly paid and their salaries were set based on a pay band, which I could not impact. This salary structure has resulted in a revolving door of people coming and going (more later on the hiring, onboarding and training processes in future chapters). While feeling appreciated by a supervisor and colleague is more highly valued for most employees than money, one thing I could affect through the swept funds process is salary. I had options to select from one-time bonuses, temporary salary adjustments, or permanent salary changes. Most of the time a permanent salary change was not an option because if I used money from one position to increase the salary for someone else's position, this left me with a salary deficit when hiring to fill a vacancy. Most of the time, I opted for bonuses and temporary salary adjustments based on exceptional efforts or increased job duties by one or more staff members due to someone leaving their position and the weight of their departure fell to the remaining staff members. I must admit, I was very successful in making that happen despite the excessive time and paperwork involved. However, just as soon as I began to understand and utilize the system to benefit my staff, the rules changed, and the changes were not communicated. We had a person resign who had been in the organization for some time and due to across the board salary increases, had a higher salary than many in the department. In an effort to reduce salary compression and level salaries for similar jobs in the department, I decided to post the salary for that same position a little lower than the previous employee in an effort to use some of the excess swept funds to make permanent salary adjustments for employees across the board, which would have had everyone paid at the same rate for similar work experience. I made this decision based on past successes within the structure only to find out well after I made the decision that now any swept funds were no longer available to me and would be moved to my supervisor on the division level. Had I known that this would have been the case, I would not have made the salary decision I did when filling this vacancy.

One time I took an administrative budget action and chose to use swept funds salary dollars from vacated positions as a bonus for each of my staff members who were taking on extra duties. All of them were going to have to take on a heavier workload until these vacated positions were filled and the new staff were trained. There wasn't much money available, but what I could use resulted in a small bonus per staff member. After all was said and done, the head of HR later called me to tell me I should have set this up as a temporary salary adjustment because that action would factor into the gross salary calculation impacting my staff members' retirement income. What?! Why didn't someone tell me this when they received my request on paper? Why wasn't it written down somewhere on the reams of paperwork I had to complete? This was a painful lesson. Of course, since then when similar circumstances have arisen, I took the appropriate action.

I'll say it again: perception is reality. Many of your staff have no idea what is involved in making these types of decisions or the amount

The Middle Child

of work involved to make something like this happen. From their point of view, money is money, and it all is spent the same way. They may be thinking or even telling you they don't understand how there isn't money to spend on professional development or occasionally buying lunch for the staff, but there is money to hire temporary employees or give people bonuses. While money does all spend the same way, the rules on how it is spent can vary depending on your organization. Be sure you understand your budget and ALL of the rules on how it can be spent. A one-hour workshop or a video made by the Human Resources department will give you an overview, but it will likely not be enough.

It is important to pick your battles in the tug of war. Early in my middle-management career when I started a new position, I was given the opportunity to purchase new furniture for our department's lobby waiting area. The new furniture was a significant upgrade from the 1970's light blue paisley-type with brass brads design. The chairs had been in that lobby for at least 10 years and were probably hand-me-downs from another department. Let me just say they were gross. I considered it a coup to be able to make this small but significant yet costly change so early in my tenure. I looked into all of the rules associated with making such a purchase and consulted all of the appropriate people to confirm the purchase was aligned and on target for an on-time delivery before the end of the fiscal year. (By the way, be sure you know when your fiscal year ends. For some organizations it is June 30, others it is September 30 and others still it is December 31). The furniture vendor assured me the chairs and side tables would be delivered and installed by June 30, which was the end of our fiscal year. When I learned this wasn't going to happen, I called the budget office to make sure the money could be encumbered into the next year only to learn that this was not permitted. No matter how many ways I tried to slice and dice the situation, the answer remained no. After speaking with my direct supervisor about it, I was told I would have to use money from next year's budget to pay for the furniture. So, I found myself in a situation where now I had a tidy sum sitting in my budget that would be absorbed into the larger organization's budget and I would have nothing to show for it AND I would be starting the next fiscal year with a significant shortfall.

In an effort to spend the money that would otherwise go unspent, I ended up assessing other needs in our department and asking the staff for a wish list of items. From there, I determined what I could purchase in the remaining days of the fiscal year and receive them in time. I made it happen. I was not going to give all of that money back. We had to be creative and think about these purchases in a strategic way. No one needs a year's worth of paperclips and staples. Besides, where would you keep it all?

Despite voicing the inefficiency of this matter, nothing changed. I just learned from it and moved on. I decided it wasn't worth irritating others to make the situation change for the future. I found a way to turn it around to benefit my staff by getting some needs and wants unexpectedly met. Ironically, I experienced almost the same dynamic years later when I was purchasing some 'swag' (pens, water bottles, padfolios, etc. with our company logo on it). I used the departmental credit card to make these purchases in early June in anticipation of supply chain delays or printing issues so that we could record that the items were received before the end of the fiscal year. While the items arrived in plenty of time, I discovered two months later that the charge for these items was on our August credit card statement instead of June. I called the vendor and was told nonchalantly that they 'always' charge two months after delivery, but if I wanted it to be charged when I placed the order, I just needed to tell them. What?! In the real world when I make a purchase with my personal credit card, my account is charged immediately. This made no sense. Nowhere on the vendor's website or invoice is there language to suggest this practice. How would I know this? So once again I found myself in a new fiscal year with a budget shortfall. Note to self: be sure to check your departmental card statement on time and with great care. Had I not been distracted by other things, I might have avoided this small calamity. Nevertheless, to help my fellow middle-managers avoid the same headaches should they use the same vendor, I gave them the heads up on this unique billing practice so they could avoid experiencing

The Middle Child

the same pain. There are countless other examples I could give in this realm but keep reading. There is more to come.

Your personal adaptability is critical to your success. Since March 2020 when the world was turned sideways due to the COVID-19 outbreak, the rules of engagement changed on a daily basis. Workplace practices had to turn on a dime and employees began working remotely, while others could not at all depending on their role.

People will only change when staying the same is more painful. COVID-19 ramped that up until it was palpable. There was a healthy undercurrent of fear and frustration, and workplace policies and procedures were changing rapidly. As a leader, you are the calming presence amidst chaos. And timely and clear communication is equally as important. COVID-19 has taught me that even though I may not know all of the answers, it's alright not to know, and we're going to figure it out. Communicate what you can and let people know as soon as possible if that information may change and when. People are more likely to hang with you when they know you have their best interest at heart. I once read that if you don't tell people what's going on, they'll make up what they don't know by talking with others in the organization. Before long, you have a gossip train a mile long and people swirling for no reason. And the worst part is that only a fraction of what is being spread has any truth.

You may be thinking, "Being a middle manager is a turnoff and a thankless job. I only want to stay in it as long as necessary to get to the next level." Or "I'm wading in the shallow end of the pool and I want to be in the deep end." Read the next chapter about developing yourself and consider your why. In the meantime, be where you are and master the skills to be a great leader in the system you're in. Affect what you can because the next rung on the career ladder comes with more responsibility and more challenging decisions. As the old adage says, "you've got to learn to walk before you can run." You must learn how to tread water, so you don't drown.

STRATEGY TIME:

1. Scrutinize the policies and procedures of your organization. Most organizations have a manual or online modules for some basic onboarding. Read them. Scour the Human Resources website and make an appointment with a knowledgeable staff member to discuss your questions. Do not accept an answer of 'it's on the website.' If you are new to your role, make it a priority to become familiar with it in your first weeks and months. I promise you, it will save you valuable time and energy, not to mention frustration.
2. Ask a lot of questions. Unfortunately, it's likely you will get little or insufficient training. Ask questions like:
    a. How are my budget dollars allocated?
    b. What are processes for encumbering money?
    c. What is the process for temporary versus permanent salary increases, if one exists? Pros/Cons of this action versus a bonus?
    d. What level of decision-making authority do I have relative to the budget? Hiring or salary decisions? How many levels of approval are there?
3. Go on a listening tour. Talk to people who have worked there a long time, especially other middle managers and your supervisor. What are the 'unwritten rules' within the organization? Speak with your Employee Relations Specialist and a Benefits Coordinators who work in Human Resources. It is likely you will get direct questions from people in your department about how various policies and procedures impact them. For example, I had a staff member who had a baby within a few months of her starting her position. She did not have enough leave accrued to remain in a paid status while on maternity leave, but I learned through my trying to help her that the company had a policy allowing

The Middle Child

staff members to apply for leave from the company sick bank. Employees could donate their leave to the sick bank even allocating to whom they wanted the leave days to go. Another place I worked allowed employees to donate leave, but they couldn't specify its recipient. Similarly, employees had to use all of their accrued annual and sick leave before applying to use sick bank days. Employees also had the ability to apply for up to five days of their own future sick days' accrual. Organizations have interesting and unique ways for addressing a variety of employee matters. It is important you know what they are so you can appropriately assist and advise your team members.

ACTION PLAN:

- In the next five days, I will:

_____

_____

_____

_____

_____

_____

- In the next 10 days, I will:

_____

_____

_____

_____

_____

_____

The Middle Child

- In the next 30 days, I will:

_____

_____

_____

_____

_____

_____

_____

- The person/people I need to talk to about this are:

_____

_____

_____

_____

_____

_____

_____

CHAPTER 4

Man in the Mirror

"If it doesn't challenge you, it doesn't change you."
– Fred DeVito

Self-de-vel-op-ment. *n.* The process by which a person's character or abilities is gradually developed. *(Oxford American Dictionary)*

Many of you reading this probably have heard of Michael Jackson and know his famous 1988 song "Man in the Mirror." In it, he sings about making the world a better place, starting with the person staring back at him in the mirror. The song's message is focused on the larger context of changing the world's problems by facing yourself first. You can dial this larger message back into your daily work life by taking the time to develop yourself. In the last chapter you worked on identifying your values, considering your leadership style and developing your leadership philosophy. My fifth-grade teacher, Mr. Parker, used to say to our class, "Good, better, best. Never let it rest, until your good is better and your better is best." I later learned that he was quoting professional basketball player, Tim Duncan. Regardless of who said it, I have never forgotten it and have said it many, many times throughout my life. As a leader, you can never be satisfied. This is not arrogance; this is humility. Good leaders know that they do not know it all and constantly strive to get better at their craft. Any professional or Olympic athlete would tell you the same.

Years ago, my husband and I took ballroom dancing lessons. As a part of our growth, we agreed to participate in the studio's annual showcase exhibition event. Think popular reality television program "Dancing with the Stars," but without all of the TV cameras, media and hype. We decided on the dance, learned the choreography, and bought the costumes and make-up. For months, we worked on our routine. My husband has a background in music, so he was a great lead. He once told me he could see the notes in his head. I remember thinking to myself, "Oh boy, am I in trouble. I can only hear the notes." As we continued to practice and the weeks rolled closer and closer to showcase time, I asked our instructor when we would be 'done' with the routine. He looked at me puzzled. I clarified by asking when the routine would be solid enough, perfect enough, to put it out on the dance floor. His response was "never." Wow. A lesson in the arts can be translated into a lesson in leadership. You are never done. And you will make mistakes. Learn from them.

> ...
>
> **If you can accept you don't know everything, then you can learn to do anything.**
>
> ...

Years ago, I attended a workshop where the speaker was talking about a mistake she had made and how she kept repeating that mistake which cost her time and money, not to mention frustration. She said her lesson was "if you don't learn from your mistakes, God will make you go through them again." Good lesson. I have tucked that nugget away. Even further, it is said that it is smart to learn from your mistakes but wise to learn from the mistakes of others. So pay attention.

This chapter will introduce you to yourself. If you want to be a great leader, you must continually grow. You must know and establish your priorities and leverage your strengths. When you are sharing what you learn through your leadership development, you are being a role model for future leaders of your department or office. As you grow in your leadership, the formal role you play in your organization may also change. Perhaps you were a front-line person and have moved into a shift manager position or assistant director role. You can no longer do your new job the way you did your previous one without changing something about yourself. If you can accept you don't know everything, then you can learn to do anything.

Assessment

For any organization to be healthy, they must assess their product, their processes and their performance. The same is true for you as a leader. There are many useful and spot-on assessments available on the market today that have little or no investment other than your time. For many of them you'll need to invest between $20 and $50 to gain access.[8] There are three in particular I have found extremely useful for me personally. They have helped me grow as a person and a leader.

Myers-Briggs Type Indicator: grounded in Carl G. Jung's theory of psychological type. Isabel Briggs Myers and her mother, Katherine Briggs, developed this instrument identifying 16 unique personality types based on personal preferences.

Extraversion(E)/Introversion (I): This is where people get their energy. Extroverts get their energy from other people, whereas introverts get their energy from within themselves. An "E" may find going to a party on a Friday or Saturday night thrilling, whereas an "I" might find this draining and would find spending the evening alone or with a few friends equally as thrilling.

Sensing (S)/Intuition(N): This is how people gather information. Do they gather their information using their five senses or do they use their intuition? A good example might be putting together a bicycle. Typically, an "S" might get the instructions and lay out the bike parts, while an "N" might try to figure out how to put the bike together using their intuition and rely on the instructions when or if necessary.

Thinking(T)/Feeling (F): This is how people make decisions. Thinkers, or "T's" make decisions using logic whereas Feelers, or "F's" make decisions using their heart and may weigh in how their decisions impact others.

Judging (J)/Perceiving (P): This is how people live or structure their lives as it relates to decisions or taking in information. "J's" tend to like structure and things decided, whereas a "P" may prefer to keep things loose and undefined should new information come forward. Js tend to live and die by their calendar. They may have already decided what they're going to order for dinner when they go to their favorite restaurant and may organize their clothes closet by color or season. A "P" preference may keep a calendar but may or may not use it in the same way a "J" preference personality might. A "P" preference may order something new every time they go to the same restaurant or may decide to try a new place at the last moment.

Upon completing the instrument, these eight dichotomy preferences are represented in 16 four-letter MBTI® types, which represents your unique approach to daily life. There is no one best type. This is a tool for leaders to leverage the knowledge they have about themselves and their team. It is a $49.95 investment. For a more enriched understanding and application of the results, I encourage you to pursue a consultation with a certified MBTI coach.

I have been a fan of the MBTI® Type Indicator since the very first time I learned about it some 30 years ago and took the assessment myself. It has been a fantastic tool for self-understanding and appreciation of differences and as I have grown and learned more about myself, I have found that it continues to be an accurate reflection of my personality preferences.

Because most of my career has been in an environment that is focused on the growth and development of young adults and people's feelings are highly regarded, I have learned to accommodate my style as necessary in my decision-making even when my personal preference would suggest otherwise. I tend to prefer making decisions quickly and with logic and data and then move on to the next thing. I also tend to be rather frank and to the point and sometimes this does not land well with others, so I have learned to adapt my style to impact my influence in my work environment. This has taken a lot of internal work and sometimes does not serve me well, but almost always it serves the people I work with well. I have also found that my MBTI® results connect nicely to my Clifton StrengthsFinder® results.

CliftonStrengths/Clifton StrengthsFinder: This instrument has been available since the 1990's and is grounded in the work by educational psychologist Donald Clifton, who was interested in the strengths of top performers. Dr. Clifton worked with The Gallup Organization in collaboration with Marcus Buckingham to develop the CliftonStrengths Assessment. The focus of this assessment is not on personality but rather on the innate talents that with self-awareness, education and coaching can become strengths, which can be performed over time to near perfect performance every time. The assessment can be used by individuals as well as work groups. The primary report is based on 34 Signature Themes and reports the Top 5 Clifton Strengths for $19.99. To get the CliftonStrengths 34, you will invest $49.99. According to Gallup, there is almost an infinite number of combinations (34^{33}); a 1:278,256 chance of having the same top 5 as someone else; and a 1:33.39 million chance of the same Top 5 in the same order.[9]

My Top 5 are Achiever, Input, Responsibility, Learning and Connectedness and the StrengthsFinder Insight Report couldn't be more spot-on. In recent years, I have taken a Strengths-based approach to our professional development activities in the office. Each staff member has taken the Clifton Strengths Finder and we have had work retreats focused on each person's specific strengths. Because I understand the language of Strengths, I am now able to put work committees together more effectively, seek out specific people in the office for feedback based on their strengths, and identify it when I see it in action. In fact, each staff member has a small 5x7 frame on their desks that holds their name and their Top 5 Strengths imprinted on it. I love this. It helps keep things in perspective and on days when someone may be getting on my nerves, I go to their Strengths first and think about whether they are approaching their work or me from their Strengths lens. Of course, the person may be operating out of their 'basement' (when strengths are overdone) and feedback may be appropriate to course correct. I can even see when I end up in my own basement. As an Achiever, I get very focused on tasks and the busier I get and the more tasks that pile up, I start to make mistakes. For me there are simply too many details to focus on. I start to send emails to the wrong person or forget to put a piece of important information in an email. It happens, without fail, two or three times a year. During those seasons, I recognize that I'm in the basement, slow down, and regain my composure so I can maximize my Achiever talent as a strength once again.

Similarly, my bottom two (out of 34 themes) are Empathy and Competition. Many of my colleagues find this difficult to believe because my daily behaviors and decisions operate from a place of caring and my colleagues perceive (and rightfully so) that I do care about people and work hard to make sure they are well cared for. I often have to explain that I am empathetic, I just don't start with empathy when making decisions. As I mentioned earlier, because my workplace environment places a high value on people's feelings, I have learned to make sure I keep them in the mix. Similarly, as an Achiever, this often comes across as competitive, but I really do not care about the competition, I care about being the best that I can be.

StandOut®: created in 2011 by New Your Times Best-Selling Author, Marcus Buckingham, and grounded in Strengths, will result in a 14-page detailed personalized report describing your greatest sources of strength and contribution.[10] At the time of this book's publication, there is no fee to take the assessment and is a great add-on assessment to the CliftonStrengths Finder.

DiSC: a personal assessment tool that promotes improved self-awareness, teamwork, communication, and productivity at work. Each letter represents four personality profile defined by the model. As described on their website[11]:

Dominance (D): places emphasis on accomplishing results and "seeing the big picture." They are confident, sometimes blunt, outspoken, and demanding.

Influence (I): places emphasis on influencing or persuading others. They tend to be enthusiastic, optimistic, open, trusting, and energetic.

Steadiness (S): places emphasis on cooperation, sincerity, loyalty, and dependability. They tend to have calm, deliberate dispositions, and don't like to be rushed.

Conscientiousness (C): places emphasis on quality and accuracy, expertise, and competency. They enjoy their independence, demand the details, and often fear being wrong.

As with the MBTI® no one DiSC style is better than the other and is preference based, as we all use each of these on any given day and in any given circumstance. More information can be found on their website and prices begin at $72.00. There are also free or lower cost options for DiSC personality testing that can be found online as well.

I first learned about this assessment when I attended a *Bud to Boss* one-day workshop after getting an internal promotion at work. As a part of this workshop, all participants took this assessment. Many years later, as part of a staff retreat, I hired an external facilitator to lead our team in DiSC related activities. (I did this because sometimes you need to be a member of the team and not always be the leader. By doing this you are being a role model in humility and learning). The staff took the free assessment in advance of the retreat and the facilitator was the only person who had the results before the event. The facilitator walked us through what each of the four personality styles were and each member of the team, including me, self-identified which style we thought we fell under. I was pretty sure I had been a D style many years prior but found myself gravitating toward a different style so moved together with others that had also identified with that style, only to find out when the facilitator revealed the results that I in fact still scored as a D style. And I was the ONLY person out of 17 who had that style. Talk about being lonely.

After the team learned the individual results, we were again assigned to small groups based on our DiSC style. Once the groups convened, we were assigned to design the layout for a fictitious new building that would house our department. Each group was sent away with a marker and a 20"x24" piece of white paper and 20 minutes to complete the task. We were told each group would report their recommendations. This was a great opportunity for team building, collaboration, and brainstorming, except perhaps for me, who sat alone. When we returned to the large group, each small group shared their ideas. Some drew pictures, some drew flowcharts, and I had a bulleted list. There was no right or wrong, but this exercise certainly illustrated how the same group of people can solve a problem in different ways. It was also a tangible way for people to see their colleagues' styles.

Keirsey Temperament Sorter: This exercise first became available through the book *Please Understand Me* by Dr. David Keirsey and Marilyn Bates in 1978 (5th edition 1984). Early publications of the book had the instrument printed in the back of the book and readers could complete it themselves. The Keirsey Temperament Sorter identifies four temperaments SP (Artisan), SJ (Guardian), NT (Rational) and NF (Idealist) and is drawn from the MBTI Personality Inventory. It is based on the idea that people's values differ from one another on a fundamental level. Today the assessment can be taken online for between $20.96 to $59.95[12].

People are complex and there is not one instrument that can quantify or capture the uniqueness of each individual person. There are many factors at play. Nevertheless, not only have I found these assessments to be spot on and personally enriching, but I have also found them to expand my appreciation for people in general and how they approach their work. I have had staff members in the past who thought all of these instruments were bunk or lacked credibility because some of their research is proprietary. However, I have tried to put these folks at ease by assuring them that I will not be putting them or any of their colleagues into a box or making substantial decisions about anything based on the information these assessments provide. My approach is simple. Come to work each day and believe that the people working with you are also coming to work each day with good intentions (even though some days it does not feel that way). These assessment results provide a much greater appreciation for the diversity of ideas, thoughts, work-patterns, and points-of-view of our colleagues, which makes our organizations better.

According to Gartner research, "only 24% of organizations today are incorporating shaping into their overall employee experience approach, yet organizations that effectively apply shaping the employee experience can achieve employees who are:
- 38% more likely to report high intent to stay
- 33% more likely to report high discretionary effort
- 44% more likely to be high performers"[13]

As leaders, we want to set up our offices and departments, as well as the people within them, for success. This starts with a leader who is humble enough to get to know themselves and give their team members the opportunity to do the same.

Priorities

Make yourself a priority. I have never been especially good at that. As an "Achiever" I am very task focused. I try to cram in as many tasks into any given hour as possible. I have high stamina and do not tire easily. This manifests itself in me often not taking the time to take a lunch hour or develop relationships with others outside my department. As I mentioned, it's not that I do not care to have those relationships, my Achiever just takes over most days. However, I got convicted of my own behavior by a friend of mine, who happened to work in our human resources department, over lunch. I was telling her a story about how my staff members were sacrificing their lunch hour to accommodate requests from our customers. These requests were often by individuals who themselves had not been responsible in making a timely appointment. I want my staff to honor their lunch hour and encourage them to do so. My friend gently pointed out to me that I was not following my own advice. She told me my staff was watching me and if I did not take a lunch, then they probably felt pressured to not take one as well. Ouch.

I still struggle with this from time-to-time, but I have gotten much better since this conversation. It's important to have people in your life who will tell you the truth and point inconsistencies out to you that you cannot see yourself.

360 Review/Coaching

About 15 years ago I had the opportunity to participate in a 360 Review. This was not part of the performance review cycle but an opportunity to solicit feedback from peers, direct reports, and any other person in the workplace you desired feedback from. Each person you identified received an email requesting feedback about your performance and behaviors in the workplace through specific questions in a survey. Those results were then aggregated and delivered to me in a comprehensive report. For the most part, my feedback was largely positive, but there was an area that shocked me. One person had indicated that some of my facial expressions during staff meetings made them feel like I was being judgmental or looking down on others. I had no idea what this person was talking about. Was this one time or every staff meeting? Of course, I to this day have no idea who wrote that comment. Happily, I had the opportunity to work with a Human Resources coach to review and scrutinize my report and focus on things I can do to improve. While my coach stressed the importance of looking at themes and consistent patterns of feedback, I could not let the one comment about my facial expressions go. I am an extrovert and very expressive. I would make a terrible poker player. My coach suggested that when there were points of discussion at staff meetings that I give voice to what I'm thinking about and be clear that this did not mean I was making a decision or a judgement. As an extroverted person, I liked this idea because I often think out loud through discussion anyway to make sense of my own thoughts. Implementing this practice was difficult for me, but I continue to do it to this day. I do not want to give anyone the impression I am behaving in a judgmental way.

If your organization or human resources office offers the opportunity for a 360 review, consider using it. Be sure you will have a coach to process the results and work with you to implement strategies for your improvement. It is important to note that you will never know who wrote what, so thank those you asked to participate regardless of whether they completed the survey. It is an exercise in humility and self-improvement.

STRATEGY TIME:

1. Never Stop Learning. Identify an area of growth. Set a goal to achieve and then pursue it. This could be through a formalized assessment or not.
2. Work on controlling your thought life. What you ingest, you express.
3. Leverage the people on your team/in your sphere of influence to better improve your leadership.

ACTION PLAN:

- In the next five days, I will:

_____

_____

_____

_____

_____

_____

- In the next 10 days, I will:

_____

_____

_____

_____

_____

_____

Man in the Mirror

- In the next 30 days, I will:

_____

_____

_____

_____

_____

_____

- The person/people I need to talk to about this are:

_____

_____

_____

_____

_____

P.S. You may be wondering if we finally did perform in the dance showcase. We did! I was shaking like a leaf when it began but couldn't have been happier with how we performed. Talk about stepping outside my comfort zone!

CHAPTER 5

A Matter of Taste

"Individual commitment to a group effort- that is what makes a team work, a company work, a society work, a civilization work." – Vince Lombardi (1913-1970), Athletic coach

"The role of culture is that it's the form through which we as a society reflect on who we are, where we've been, where we hope to be." – Wendell Pierce, Actor

"Culture is the habit of being pleased with the best and knowing why." – Henry van Dyke, Author

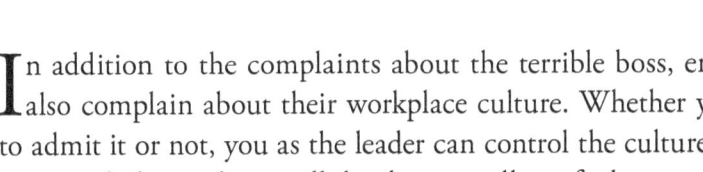

In addition to the complaints about the terrible boss, employees also complain about their workplace culture. Whether you want to admit it or not, you as the leader can control the culture because your workplace culture will develop regardless of what you do or do not do to create it, so be intentional. There are many reasons this is valuable for you to understand as a middle manager because the larger culture of the organization is also impacting your office or department.

Nevertheless, you can make the culture of your office what you want and need it to be, but this takes leadership. Having a workplace culture in which everyone is operating with the same set of norms, expectations and workplace behaviors, creates a greater opportunity to make navigating future change easier, getting greater employee buy-in and reducing opportunities for conflict. So, if you do nothing, then nothing will change. The office culture will develop and be controlled by the undefined leaders: the people that hang out in the break room and gossip; the people that talk unfavorably about their colleagues behind closed doors; the people that triangulate communication; the people that send snarky emails. You know who I'm talking about. We have all worked with these types of people. Perhaps at one time, we were these people. This makes for a very unpleasant place to work, where distrust and disengagement abound, and people start pointing fingers and dissect who is working harder than whom.

As the leader, you set the tone and the pace for the department. Your goal is increased teamwork and productivity. You want an environment where the mission and vision are at the forefront, and everyone understands why they are there and how their role in that mission and vision connects to others in the office and ultimately the people you serve.

Some great sit-coms over the decades that highlight office culture are the *Mary Tyler Moore Show*, *WKRP in Cincinnati*, *TAXI*, and *M*A*S*H*, but the one that most readers today may recognize if not resonate with is the popular 2005 television show *The Office*, starring Steve Carrell. The reason this show is popular is because every viewer recognizes the characters in the show from their own workplace experiences. Even today, many years later, the show remains in syndication. A whole new generation is being introduced to the Dunder Mifflin Paper Company. If you're not familiar with the program, let me briefly introduce you to the characters:

Michael Scott (Regional Manager): The Boss. Manipulative. Impulsive. Abuses his power. Ringleader of office shenanigans. Wants to be liked by others and attempts to endear his colleagues by using inappropriate jokes and language and justifies his actions by declaring

A Matter of Taste

he is the boss. He is easily influenced by the women he is with. He is the most frequent topic of conversation between employees behind closed doors and in the break room. Despite this, everyone in the office loves him. His quirks are endearing and his desire to be liked shows up in odd ways.

Dwight (Assistant to the Regional Manager): Has a God Complex and believes he should be the boss. Does not understand social cues. Specific about his concerns. Does whatever he wants without consequences. Is a co-conspirator in Michaels's shenanigans and often sucks up to Michael.

Jim (Salesperson): Probably the most 'normal' of the workgroup. Doesn't put up with crap. Stands by and watches things happen. Sometimes he participates in office shenanigans if he thinks it is funny or will mess with Dwight.

Pam Beesley (Secretary): Quiet and submissive. Occasionally tries to keep Michael in line. Eventually moves up the ranks to salesperson. Later in the series marries Jim and has a child.

Andy Bernard (Salesperson): Optimist of the group. Personally hurt when Michael gets on his case.

Stanley Hudson (Salesperson): Shows up for work and does what he's supposed to do. Not immersed in the culture. Thinks Michael's shenanigans are crazy. Only participates in the company events when forced.

Kevin Malone (Accountant): Goof ball. People wonder how he got a job there. Still thinks potty humor is funny (alongside Michael). Child-like demeanor. Everyone thinks he is the dumb one.

Angela Martin (Lead Accountant): Eventually gets in a relationship with Dwight. Thinks she is the smartest of the bunch and thinks everyone there is dumb except her. Head of the party planning committee. Strick and stuck in her ways. Pessimist of the group. Mean cat lady. OCD. Sticks close to her morals or values. She gets very upset when people offend her sensibilities (this comes through in her party planning).

Oscar (Accountant): Collateral damage in Michael's shenanigans.

Toby (Head of Human Resources): He is Michael's conscience. Therefore, Michael hates him.

Creed (Quality Control): A Background character. He's there and he's not all the same time. Kind of creepy.

Meredith (Supplier Relations): Takes opportunities to take her shirt off. Strong personality. Flamboyant. Bed pals with Dwight.

I never watched this show when it first premiered. In fact, the first time I ever saw an episode was at a staff development activity planned by our department's Staff Development Committee at the end of a very stressful and busy season. They selected an episode in which Michael challenged Dwight to a sumo wrestling match at a nearby dojo. As I watched this calamity unfold over the next 20 minutes, I was absolutely mortified. Meanwhile, I'm attempting to not display my shock and dismay over Michael's behavior and that the entire office would play along by attending the event.

I think you may get my point here. Michael had no intention and likely never considered his office culture or frankly, probably never gave it a second thought. As a result, the culture developed into a toxic, dysfunctional, and unproductive environment.

It's a story people know and live every day. This chapter will discuss how to create and sustain an agreed upon work culture in your office. Whether you are new to your position or have been in your position for many years, it is never too late to change your office culture for the better. Culture is directly related to having the right people in the right roles and we will address how to find those people in a future chapter. In the meantime, you can develop the culture you desire with the people you have onboard right now.

At the end of the day, the key factor in any healthy workplace culture is trust. If your people do not trust you or each other, it is like walking through three feet of snow without snowshoes. For most people, you have to earn their trust and trust is complicated. It could take a week or years to gain someone's trust and lose it in an instant with poorly chosen words or actions. Someone's ability to trust isn't necessarily based on you as the leader, but it does impact their interactions with you. It's based on their personal experiences both in and out of the workplace. The good news is you're only human and the sun comes up each day for a 'do-over,' if needed. If you violate someone's trust, you must have the humility to apologize and make it right.

Several years ago, within three weeks of one another, both my daughter and my husband each experienced a very serious health crisis, and it impacted the very foundation of our family life and shook us to our core. Needless to say, I was worried, stressed and distracted. Thankfully, they both are now doing great; however, when I reflect back on that time, I realize that while I came to work every day and did my absolute best, I think some of my staff took advantage of the fact that I was highly distracted. On top of my personal distractions, our office simultaneously had several staff position vacancies. Due to the time of year, I had no one to delegate the duties that were left by the vacancies; so for better or worse, I ended up doing them myself, which was a further distraction. I was managing instead of leading. Over that period, I lost my handle on our office culture. Some of the people in the office found joy in fanning the flames of discontent and started to create an environment of distrust and escalating points of conflict, which only made matters worse. The water cooler conversations became complaint sessions. As you have probably experienced yourself, most people are savvy enough not to have these conversations in front of their supervisor, but when I had people come report these activities were occurring and when I asked them what they did about it, the typical response was they simply didn't participate. I appreciated it, but they also didn't STOP it. This could be because they either did not know how to address it or were afraid to do so. On some level, who could blame them? They could end up being the next topic of conversation. I knew I had a big problem on my hands. It is extremely difficult to address what you do not see but know is happening. If you address it because of hearsay, you could be talking to the wrong person. If you don't address it at all, the behavior continues, and your environment continues to erode. Either way, your moral authority is in jeopardy and it is your fault if it does not change.

Another issue I had for many years prior to this problem was regular staff attrition due to low pay or no opportunity for advancement. By default, with each person's departure, you as the leader have to start all over again reestablishing mutual trust, creating community and shared experiences. As a part of my strategy to change my department's culture, I decided I needed to create opportunities for my people to position themselves to take on more formal responsibility through a next level position instead of leaving the department or moving elsewhere in the organization. Because my hands were tied on matters related to creating new salary dollars, I used what I knew about the HR salary and classification practices to change the job duties for existing vacant positions and reclassify them within the larger HR guidelines. These new positions would shape my leadership team and resulted in a new reporting structure. The result of the decision to reorganize meant I had both internal and external applicants.

Once my leadership team had been hired and was in place, I worked with an external consultant to help build trust and community within this newly established team. The selection and hiring process netted two internal hires and two new external members of this new team. As a part of this experience, we spent time sharing our career histories and identifying shared values with one another. We later focused on what kind of values we wanted for the larger team. While some leadership materials suggest all values should come from the team, I decided that we were at a critical juncture. I decided that some of our values would be negotiable, but others were not. The leadership team decided team spirit, accountability, and humility were our 'non-negotiables.' Then we spent time defining what each of these values WAS and what it WAS NOT with specific behavior-based language. For example, team spirit is 'being willing to participate' but is not 'not being willing to disclose one's point of view.' Humility is 'being willing to share feedback to others in a respectful way,' but it is not 'not willing to reflect on opportunities to improve.' Accountability is 'consistent expectations for all group members,' but it is not 'inconsistent messaging from leadership.'

From this point forward, I was very strategic in how the rest of our office culture 're-set' would unfold. We started a series of staff meetings, retreats and workshops over the next twelve months that would set the stage for what I hoped to be a collective shared future. The first in this series was a staff meeting about who I am and where I came from. I likened myself to that of a conductor of a symphony with each person on our staff playing his or her own instrument in our orchestration. I also revisited our department's mission and vision. While it may feel weird to do so, you cannot keep this in front of your staff enough. A sign on the wall in the copy room or in the main lobby is not enough to motivate people. Your department's mission and vision are the WHY of your work's existence. You can revisit this at staff meetings, where appropriate, in one-on-one conversations, or connect it to a decision you make. You should also consider including your department's cultural values in all performance related discussions throughout the year from goal setting to progress updates.

During this staff meeting I had a healthy potted plant on the desk near me alongside a bedraggled plant barely hanging on to life. I talked about how each plant has very specific needs and in order for them to grow they need a healthy environment. They need a proper-sized pot, the correct soil, sunlight and water levels. As humans, we need this too. Each of us has different needs and the goal of that day's activity and our future retreats and workshops would be designed to help us all thrive. I shared my expectations of them for our collective shared future. I said I expected everyone to approach their colleague's behavior with positive regard. I have met very few people in my working life who wake up in the morning and think about how they can piss someone off when they come into work. That's not to say there isn't inappropriate behavior that needs to be addressed, but for the most part I think people have good intentions. No one is perfect after all; they're just being who they are. I said I expected people to abide by the departmental guidelines and policies and explained why. I also highlighted that not everything is as it seems. We all use our own perceptions and filters to make meaning of what we see happening around us. Perception is reality, so instead of making assumptions, ask questions when they are unclear or unsure. I went on to share what they can expect from me.

Leadership in the Trenches

To symbolically close out this staff meeting, I gave everyone a blank envelope and a piece of blank paper. I talked about a Death and Dying course I took in graduate school in which we discussed how 'unfinished business' prevents us from living happy lives. A graveyard is filled with people buried with their unfinished business. This could be past hurts, unforgiveness, anger, frustration…simply fill in the blank. It is different for each of us. I told everyone that I wanted them to go back to their office and write down any unfinished business they had with anyone in our department or elsewhere in the organization. If they didn't have any unfinished business with a colleague, then they could focus on something in their personal life. I told them when they finished their letter, to fold it, put it in the envelope and seal it. I could feel the distrust of some of my staff members as they asked me who would be reading what they wrote. I assured them that no one would be reading their letter and asked that they trust me. As you can imagine, this was a major trust exercise for some of them. Before they departed the space, I held up my own personal letter in a sealed envelope to show them I had already completed the task. (Remember, the leader always goes first). As a point of reference, this letter was real for me. I had some staff members who were downright mean to me and had created some serious and unnecessary strife for me. This exercise was designed as much for them as it was for me. I planned this exercise to last about 20 minutes but was willing to spend as much time as it took. I told everyone to return to the staff meeting space when they were finished with their letter. For the most part, it took about as long as I had planned.

While the staff went back to their personal office spaces to work, I took one of the office shredders and perched it on a table in our meeting space. Once everyone had returned, I explained that we would each be shredding our grievances, unforgiveness, unspoken concerns and were going to let them go. No longer would we be held prisoner to this unfinished business and we are all expected to no longer let it interfere with our office relationships. We would only be moving forward from here.

A Matter of Taste

To close out the meeting, I introduced the forthcoming Values Survey and the next steps in our office restructure and culture re-set. The values survey was an anonymous electronic survey distributed after the meeting to all members of the staff. It included a list of about 15 possible value options, including a write-in option. I outlined for the staff the three standing non-negotiable values of team spirit, accountability and humility and the staff will identify an additional three. The reason I decided on six total values is because it is manageable. There are enough to remember and make meaningful. I thought six was also enough that it would force prioritization in the decision-making by the staff. The more people you have on a team, the larger the value spectrum.

The forthcoming new reporting lines were also an area of worry for some on my staff. I did my best to assure the entire team that I was being thoughtful about who would be reporting to whom, but the intention behind this decision was so that they could get better care and have more intentional and systematic opportunities to provide feedback. As part of the decision, I told them I was thinking about gender balance, years of experience in their role, strengths of each staff member including the team leader, office dynamics, and opportunities for growth, development, and synergy.

The next step was our "reveal" retreat. We started the day off with a Common Ground ice breaker, which is designed for the members of the team to learn more about what they had in common. Each staff member was given an index card and asked to write down one fun or interesting fact about themselves they thought no one else knew. This would be a challenge for some because some of the people in the room had worked together for more than 10 years. As each person completed the task, I asked them to put their index card in a bowl at the front of the room. When all cards had been deposited in the bowl, I asked for a volunteer who would be willing to start us off by selecting a random card, reading it aloud and then guessing who the card belonged to. If the card they selected was their own, I asked them to return it to the bowl. If their guess was wrong, the group jumped in to help until the person's fun fact was connected to the correct person. All of the index cards were attached to a large sticky note on an easel, and we identified a key element or theme for each person's fun fact and captured this on a separate large sticky note. If you decide to do this exercise, try to stick to just one or two words for each person's fun fact. Then we brainstormed common themes, words, or phrases from all of the key words and documented these on a separate large sticky note. I then asked people to pair up with the person beside them and produce a tag line for the group. Each pair shared their idea and again this was captured on a large sticky note. As a large group, we collectively decided on a group tag line. This was fun, light-hearted, and enlightening activity and a small step toward building community and trust. Our tagline was later publically displayed in our mail room.

After this activity, we revealed the results of the Values Survey. First, I talked about our three non-negotiable values and gave examples of what they ARE and what they AREN'T. Then I shared a PowerPoint slide with real time survey results and the top three were very clear: communication, appreciation, and inclusiveness. Before the retreat, I wrote each of the additional values at the top of a 20"x 36" large sticky note. The value was written at the top and a line was drawn at the halfway mark vertically down the center creating two columns. On the left was written "what it IS" and on the right was written "what it ISN'T." As I was giving instructions for the next activity, I secured these large sticky notes to the wall in three different spots in the room. Then I gave each staff member a small stack of sticky notes. The instructions for this activity had each person write one behavior per sticky note for each value and each column. They could write as many as they wanted and could be supplied with more sticky notes if needed. Once each person felt like they had exhausted their ideas, they were to take their sticky notes and place them in the appropriate column for each of the three identified values.

When all the staff members were finished, each large sticky note was removed from the wall and attached to an easel. Then we went about the task of reviewing each sticky note in each column for each value and grouping like behaviors together. Clarification was sought

A Matter of Taste

for any sticky notes that were unclear. Then we went about the business as a group discussing and describing for the team the "what it IS" and "what it ISN'T" for each value. It was a very organic process and we took as much time as we needed.

Keep in mind, as the leader and retreat facilitator, you need to be mindful of how people are feeling and the pace of the event. You also have to be mindful of how you are feeling as well. Remember, you have your own perceptions and filters and as you work through the process, you must work hard not to internalize what a value IS and ISN'T as a personal criticism. However, truth be told, I know there were lessons for me as the leader in this and I needed to role model our newly established value of Humility.

After a lunch break, I spent time revisiting our mission and vision as well as our organization's history, accomplishments, and where we were going. Each member of the leadership team talked about their specific job duties and their goals for their role to grow the area of the department for which they were each responsible, and I shared the new structure for our future staff meetings. Two times a month, we would meet as a large group and two times a month we would meet as small groups. The outcomes for the small group meetings included a continued discussion about our departmental core values; accountability to those values through established personal goals; accountability and commitment to established group goals; discussion about policies, processes, and feedback about our work. Lastly, each team leader would meet one-on-one with each member of their team. This could be during the designated time for small groups or at another agreed upon time. Then it was time for the small group teams to be revealed (with some fanfare I might add).

After a short break, the small groups convened for a community building activity in which members of the group shared a brief career history highlighting their first professional job, other positions that they've held, what they liked/disliked about those jobs, what they learned about themselves, how long they have been in their current role, what they're most proud of to date, and how they are interested in growing and developing in their current role. During this time, each team leader gave their small group a Value Vision Worksheet as 'homework.' This was due before the next small group meeting a couple of weeks later. This homework required each staff member to think about what they would want to personally achieve in relation to each stated value and then commit to intentionally work on it over the next three months.

The closing activity for the day is what I call the Plant Activity. I gave each staff member a hot pink index card and a neon green index card. I asked each staff member to write on the hot pink card any remaining negative feelings or burdens. On the neon green card, I asked them to write what they were excited about, positive feelings, and hopes for the future. While they were working, I put a small plant, a new spade, some potting soil, and a large pot that I had purchased in advance of the retreat on the table where I was standing.

After they finished, I picked up a garbage can and asked them to tear up their hot pink cards and put them in the trashcan (this circled back to the Unfinished Business activity). I talked about how harsh feelings and unspoken hurts burden the individual and the team and our newfound values will be our guide. The neon green cards are our future, and these are the things that will help us grow. I reminded them of the plant illustration from a couple of weeks prior and that our goal is to thrive moving forward. I asked each person to bring their neon index card to the front and put it in the pot and using the spade cover it with some soil and then pass it to the next person. As these cards decompose over time, they will be nourishment to the plant to help it grow and thrive.

To my surprise, one of my staff members suggested we give the plant a name. What a great idea! The staff decided its name would be "Vision," which was later written on the pot itself and displayed in the lobby of our office.

POST RETREAT AND NEXT STEPS:

About a week after the retreat, we sent around another anonymous survey to the staff asking to what extent they believed they were already exemplifying the newly established office values and to what extent they believed their colleagues were displaying these same values. These results were shared at the next staff meeting.

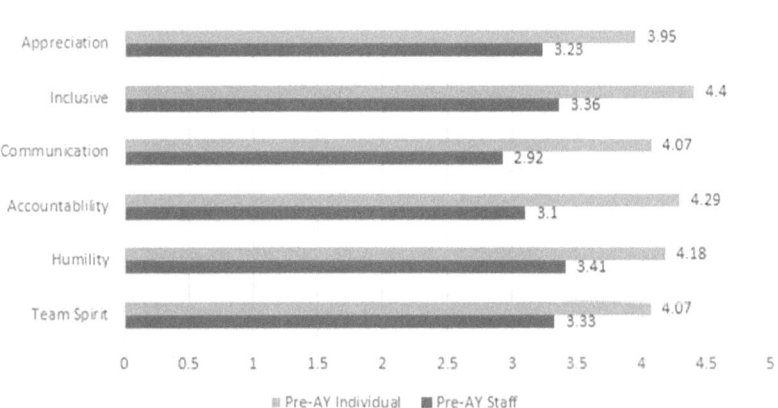

Image created by John Sare

This image reveals that, collectively, the staff perceived themselves as displaying departmental values much higher than their perception of how they thought their colleagues displayed the same values. As one of my staff members said when the information sunk in, "We sure do think a lot of ourselves."

Clearly, we had more work to do.

Over the next nine months, we had monthly professional development activities as a part of our large team meetings. These were led by a member of the leadership team around each of our new organizational values. In addition to this, we had one more half-day workshop with our same external facilitator. This workshop focused on interpersonal communication and giving and receiving feedback.

In the meantime, in an effort for staff members to recognize one another's efforts in exemplifying our newly articulated values, we used a bulletin board in our mail room to create a tree made out of construction paper. Each value was written on one branch of the tree. In two small boxes near our mailboxes, staff members would find green leaves cut out of construction paper in one and a small slip of paper where they could write their name, their colleague's name and what they witnessed from them that supported our values. With each completed acknowledgement, the staff member who completed it would staple a green leaf to the branch of the tree that represented the value displayed. The goal was that over the course of the following months the tree would go from being barren to fully blossomed. This activity gave staff members the opportunity to give feedback in a positive and low stakes way and encourage the further solidification of our values in our culture.

Needless to say, there were moments when this was extremely difficult and uncomfortable, but the rewards to come are so worth it. The goal of this culture re-set is to drive your organization's culture in a positive and productive direction and to make it so strong that those that don't buy-in to the process will either jump on board or jump ship, which is probably a good thing. Otherwise, they will be miserable and likely make those around them miserable as well. This will make building your culture even harder, but it could make having difficult conversations easier because the culture has set the expectation. You have also equipped your staff to confront inappropriate behaviour. This makes it harder for those that like to 'stir the pot' to find someone with a spoon.

After the nine-month period ended, we redistributed the same survey to the staff and happily, we saw an improvement:

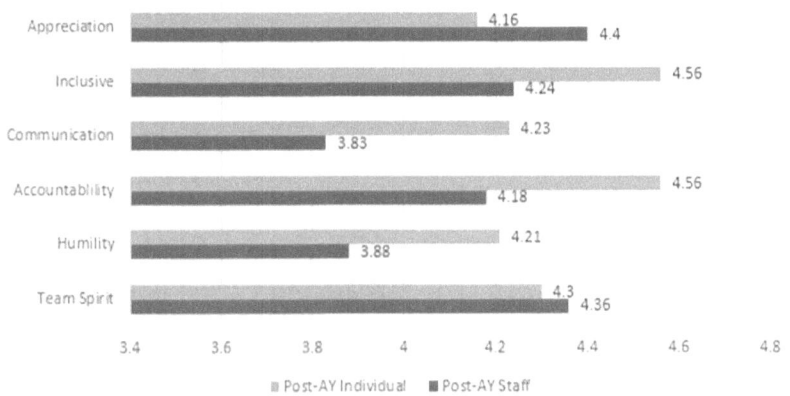

Image created by John Sare

As you can see between the two charts, we saw an increase in every category from September 2019 to June 2020. Certainly, the necessity to change business processes due to the COVID pandemic impacted some of our increases, but there is no doubt in my mind that our efforts in this area made our workplace culture so much more positive and enriching.

STRATEGY TIME:

1. Evaluate where your department's culture stands now. Does it need a re-set, or does it need to be revisited or reignited?
2. Consider your skill set to lead these activities? Do you need more training? Do you need to hire an outside consultant to facilitate a workshop or activity for your team?
3. Think about how your newly established departmental values can be infused into your daily work, communication, printed materials, even performance reviews and professional development. Where are the logical first stops?
4. Live it out daily. This is part of your moral authority.

ACTION PLAN:

- In the next five days, I will:

- In the next 10 days, I will:

Leadership in the Trenches

- In the next 30 days, I will:

  _____

  _____

  _____

  _____

  _____

  _____

- The person/people I need to talk to about this are:

  _____

  _____

  _____

  _____

  _____

  _____

CHAPTER 6

Needle in a Haystack

"The secret to my success is that we've gone to exceptional lengths to hire the best people in the world." – Steve Jobs, co-founder, chief executive and chairman of Apple Computer

Do you ever feel like finding a new team member is like searching for a needle in a haystack? Far too little time and care is taken in hiring the right person for a position. I'm going to tell you right now, doing it well is not a quick process and a one-hour interview is likely not enough if you do not do your due diligence to get the right people to the interview table. It is a very time-consuming process. You want to maximize your time before, during and after the interview and this takes careful planning. Laszlo Bock, Co-founder and CEO of Humu and Author of *Work Rules* says, "Hiring is the most important people function you have, and most of us aren't as good at it as we think. Refocusing your resources on hiring better will have a higher return than almost any training program you can develop."

Not taking the time to select the best fit candidate is a recipe for workplace disaster resulting in frustration for both parties and a lot of energy managing someone who isn't the right person for your department's culture. This impacts the team morale and ultimately results in the person leaving the organization, likely mad and disgruntled and blaming you. (Yes, it is in part your fault for not front loading the process to find the right person). Just because someone can do the job does not mean you should hire them. As Sue Tetzlaff says in *The Employee Experience: A Capstone Guide to Peak Performance*, "if you can hire tough, you can manage easy."

It is expensive to replace a vacancy. According to Zippia: the Career Expert, the average rate in 2022 to replace an employee is $4,425 with 75% of hires costing less than $4,669. Zippia further reports that it costs an average of $98 a day until a position is filled and can take up to six months for this money to be recouped if spent hiring a new person.[14] Therefore, you do not want to leave the selection to chance. This chapter will explore how to write effective position descriptions, behaviour-based interviewing practices and how to effectively evaluate candidates. This process should be intentional and should not be rushed. Before you begin, revisit your department's values and culture. Ask yourself what gaps were left by the person you are replacing or consider this an opportunity to expand the scope of the position as I discussed in an earlier chapter.

Attracting the candidates you're looking for starts with the advertisement for the vacancy and usually involves the position description. Even if your organization has rules about what can or must be included in the position description, be sure you understand how much liberty you have to customize it to your needs. Also be sure to ask who is responsible for advertising the vacancy. Does your human resources department do it? If so, where will a candidate find it? Are you given a budget for advertising the posting? This can be very expensive if you use formal avenues like professional publications, but you may also be able to use social media outlets to advertise the position. Over the years, I have learned to do better and better each time with the language I use in a position announcement. In addition to the standard resumé, cover letter and references, we began to require applicants to submit an Advising Philosophy, an idea that came from one of my colleagues during a search committee meeting. Adding this additional element made a profound difference on future applicants for positions we had. First and foremost, it ruled out a significant number of applicants who had no idea what an Advising Philosophy was and did not want to take the time to investigate otherwise. Therefore, the candidate either did not submit one or what they did submit was so poorly written, I was not willing to consider them. What was further shocking was the number of applicants that had a stellar resumé and a pitiful cover letter or advising philosophy. If past performance is an indicator of future performance, can you imagine what kind of work these folks might produce? The unexpected outcome was we had applicants that did take the time to submit thoughtful application materials, including the philosophy statement. Without the thoughtful cover letter and advising philosophy, we may have missed an applicant as their direct experience would not have had their resumé surface to the top of the pile. Needless to say, this was not a foolproof application process, but it did reduce the number of applicants that had no business applying for our position in the first place.

During the virtual EntreLeadership Summit, one of the sessions led by author and radio host, Ken Coleman, was about attracting, acquiring and retaining talent. Ken talked about creating a narrative for the position to attract the right person. I loved this idea and a lightbulb went off. I took that teaching back to my office and had small groups brainstorm the language for our narrative. Now, in addition to our job duties, we have written a narrative that includes commentary about what a successful candidate would love about the position, followed by relevant and important tasks or components. In the job position section for required knowledge, skills and abilities, I list these things under the header "Skills Required for Success in the Position." What I learned from that session is that our job announcement needed to be ultra-clear to the candidate. Dave Ramsay describes this as 'winning' on the job. I love that. Who doesn't want someone who wants to be successful in their role?

Remember that in many cases what is written in the position description will later be used as part of performance reviews, so you want to make sure the language best reflects the nature of the work. I recommend you revisit the position description at least once a year to confirm that the job duties are still accurate. Depending on what sector you lead in, you may be limited in your ability to modify too much in a job description as it relates to the key results or responsibilities found therein. Many of those factors may have been decided by an entity much older or larger than the one you find yourself. However, this is a good time to talk with your HR representative about what you can and cannot change and what flexibility or approvals you need to secure.

Most job descriptions for management positions never include the words like 'lead, leader, or team." This may be because when job descriptions are created, they are created by Human Resource practitioners who are working to make sure the language stays within job categories, bands, or levels, in an effort to equalize the work performed by any one individual within those categories and to ensure that the work is equably compensated.

As I have mentioned earlier, my department suffers from high staff turnover due to low salaries and limited opportunities to move up. This has afforded me plenty of opportunities over the years to dissect the position description as well as the selection process.

For each vacancy, it was not uncommon to have between 80-100 applicants for a single vacancy posting. Our human resources candidate application system was not sophisticated enough to rule out candidates that did not meet the minimum requirements for the position, which resulted in every member of the search committee looking at each application. Without fail we had at least a third and up to one-half of the applicants that did not meet the minimum requirements. According to Legaljobs in a February 2021 article, "An astonishing 85% of people lie on their resumés."[15] With that in mind, you cannot leave your interview process to chance.

The Search Committee

It is important to distinguish who is responsible for making the hiring decision and the difference between feedback and decision making. Be sure to research your human resources hiring guidelines and practices. Are you, as the leader in your department, the hiring manager — the person making the final decision? How much input and feedback do you want or are allowed to accept from others outside the search committee? How will you solicit and use any feedback in your decision?

Determining who should be on the search committee is another matter you need to consider. Again, what are the expectations, if any, from your human resources department? Is there a minimum number of search committee members expected? What do you need to consider in the committee's make-up? Do you need an odd or even number on the committee? Is the gender or race of the member a requirement? Do you have to have someone external from your department on the committee? Do committee members have to be approved by human resources? Or someone else? Is the search committee the deciding body or do they just recommend a candidate to the hiring manager? Or to you as the leader? It is important to have all of these questions answered before proceeding so you are clear and can give clear instructions to this group. Once you have your committee members identified and approved, if required, I recommend you schedule a meeting with the committee and give them a 'charge.' A charge would include your expectations for the search process, the kinds of skills, abilities and knowledge a future employee would demonstrate, and a timeline for completion. I also recommend you speak to the importance of strict confidentiality in the process. The last thing you need to manage is someone chatting up their colleague at the office photocopier about the candidate pool or a recent interview.

Selecting the Best Candidates to Interview

Once you have your candidates, you decide which candidates you want to interview. In general, I recommend you interview three candidates for each vacancy. While I think these should be in person, COVID-19 gave us no other choice and we have successfully offered virtual interviews in the meantime. In-person interviews provide an opportunity for the person to see your space, meet your people and get the 'vibe' of your workspace. You also get to see how the person behaves both formally and informally.

To determine the candidates you are going to interview, I recommend you create a rubric listing the criteria for the position using at least the minimum job duties. Give each candidate a score based on to what extent the candidate meets the criteria. For example, if you have a minimum number of years of experience or there is a specific skillset you're seeking, make each skill its own point for scoring. You could use a three-point scale: 1 for no/little experience, a 2 for some experience, and a 3 for extensive experience. Each member of your search committee should score each candidate independently and record a total score for each candidate. The goal of this scoring exercise is to take the emotion out of the decision and base the decision on what the candidate brings to the table when compared to the skills and experiences you are seeking. To determine which candidates you'll invite to the interview in advance of the search committee meeting, ask each committee member to provide the Chair their top three candidates from the candidate pool. This should be based on the score that they generated from the rubric when scoring the candidates.

The committee chair should collect these data from the committee members and indicate the top three candidates from each committee member on a separate document and share with the committee. This is both effective and efficient. In most cases, if the committee members used the rubric appropriately, the committee will have agreed on one if not two of the top candidates. If that is the case, then the committee will only need to discuss further the remaining candidates to interview. Of course, this is your search. You can interview as many candidates as you like, unless your organization's policy dictates otherwise. If you have many qualified and interesting candidates, you may want to start with 20-minute telephone interviews and then decide who to invite to your in-person or virtual interview. You may decide you only want to interview two candidates, and, in some cases, you may want to interview four or five.

As I mentioned earlier, I do not believe one hour is really enough time to get to know someone and determine if they're a right fit in terms of the experience, competencies, and values. The process I recommend is at least a half a day. One interview with the Search Committee for about 1-1.5 hours. Be sure you are clear on any Human Resources expectations about who should be on the interview committee before proceeding. This interview is where the committee dives into the questions that will get at the competencies and values you are seeking. Schedule an additional one hour interview with members from your team. This session is to give your team an opportunity to get to know the candidate more informally. And finally, another interview with the Director or Manager for 30 minutes to an hour. This gives the candidate the opportunity to ask questions of the department's leader and for the Director to ask specific questions, especially as it relates to the departmental values. I recommend these questions are more about fit in the office and their attitude about your work. Each of these interviews must ask different questions of the candidate. One of the worst things you can do to your candidate is waste their time by asking them the same questions by different groups of people all day long.

Once you decide who you are interviewing, be sure you follow the appropriate Human Resources practices. You may need to get appropriate approvals before inviting candidates to the interview. While you are awaiting administrative approvals, block out time on the calendars of everyone involved so you can schedule the interviews. You may need to do this as soon as you have candidates identified because folks tend to have very full calendars.

Once you contact the candidates and set up their interview, follow up with the candidate confirming the date, time, location or virtual internet link, as well as the schedule for the day of the interview, including staff members involved. One of the elements that I added to our process is to send each candidate we are interviewing a "Candidate Packet." This packet includes information about the organization, its mission, and organizational structure. It also includes information about our department including our vision, mission, departmental org structure, our departmental values, committees, and other cool information about the city where we live. These are the types of things a candidate most likely will not find on your website.

Writing Great Interview Questions

Another way to waste your candidate's and staff's time is by asking questions that will not solicit the information you need. Questions like "If you could be any animal, what animal would you be and why? Or "What sports team do you follow?" may be interesting, but they are irrelevant to whether the person could do the job.

The most popular interview question is "Tell me about yourself." This is a decent question and most candidates are prepared to answer it, but in my experience most of the time the candidate just tells me what they wrote on their resumé. A better question might be, "You wrote in your cover letter you…. Tell me about why you have applied for this position." I always close an interview session with the search committee by asking, "What do you hope to gain from this position that you do not already have?" I ask this because I am interested in the candidate's goals for professional growth. If they cannot answer this question, you may want to consider if this is the candidate for you.

As you are preparing questions, be sure you know what questions you can NOT ask. Questions about race, age, citizenship, gender, sexual orientation, religion, disability, marital status, and whether the candidate has children or plans to have children are illegal. Many years ago, I was interviewing for a position. I was already married at that time but had not yet had children. The woman that was interviewing me laughingly said to me that she "hoped I didn't have any immediate plans to have children." I sat there in shock and dismay. I really needed this job and was suddenly feeling very uncomfortable. I bypassed her comment by trying to change the subject.

Once I learned about Behavior-based Interviewing (BBI), I never looked back. The premise for BBI is that past behavior is indicative of future behavior in a similar situation. You will never see a question that will result in a yes/no answer. If you are not currently using BBI as a method for your interview process, I strongly encourage you to take the time to learn more about it and then decide to involve your staff in developing a process. It is time well spent and could be done in a two-hour workshop or staff meeting.

Needle in a Haystack

First, consider the knowledge, skills and abilities, and competencies necessary for successful job performance. This will result in a list of 5-10 skills for success that your team would be developing questions around. Then determine the Technical and Performance Skills necessary for the job. A Technical Skill may be *use of software programs* or *create technical manuals explaining procedures* and a Performance Skill may be *communication, flexibility* or *managing conflict*. Next, from each skill, develop questions that would elicit a response from the candidate about past desired job-related behaviors. An example for a Customer Service Performance Skill would be "This job involves dealing with difficult customers/clients. Tell me about a specific situation in which you had to deal with a difficult customer/client." An example of a Technical Skill for Administration may be "Tell me about a time when you had a hard deadline and had many competing priorities and how you handled it." Questions like "Tell me about a time..." or "Give me an example..." are a good place to start. BBI defines it as asking "STAR" questions: Situation, Task, Action and Results. These include questions that begin with Why, What and How. You want to get at what the candidate has already done and how those experiences will connect to the job they are applying for in your office, not what they *would* do. It's too easy to pontificate here.

Break your staff into small groups and after they have taken the time to brainstorm, bring everyone back to the large group and have small groups report back their list and solicit additions. It is likely you might find some overlap between competencies, so you'll have to decide if they need to be under one Technical Skill or under multiple.

Once competencies have been agreed upon, then you can get to the business of creating behavior-based questions for each competency area. You want to develop a set of questions for each competency area. You may or may not ask every question in each set. This is sometimes hard for members of a search committee to swallow because they see a large set of questions and become overwhelmed. As the leader, it is important you explain "Why" you are moving in this direction and the time on the front end of the process is an investment in the future for the department.

One of the great things about the BBI process is that as the interview continues, the candidate will often answer questions in other competency areas. So, while you may have way more questions than you would ever ask, you have a question bank at the ready. Generally speaking, as the candidate continues to answer questions and is checking all of your boxes, you may find as the interviewer you begin to have a positive feeling about this person. This is good but can be dangerous. Be sure to ask contrasting questions in which the candidate did not perform well or there was a painful experience. There have been times I have skipped over this piece because it feels a bit 'icky,' and I have regretted it. I find that omitting contrasting information was more about my feelings of being uncomfortable than asking the candidate a question in which they have to answer a question requiring they talk about a time when things did not go so well. Another great thing about the BBI process is that the question set does not let the candidate off the hook for answering the question. If you ask a question and you are not satisfied with their response, ask another question from that question set. Do not move on to the next competency area until you are satisfied that the question has been answered well enough for the folks on your committee to effectively evaluate and score.

The final piece of the BBI process is to create a benchmark scoring system for the candidate's responses in each of the competency areas. There should be an Exceed Expectations (score of 3), Meets Expectations (score of 2), and Below Expectations (score of 1); or a Good, Average, and Poor. In each of these scoring sections, you will need to develop responses you would expect to hear from a candidate that would exceed, meet or fall below what you would expect of a candidate. The general thought is that Knowledge, Skills, and Abilities are written at the Meets/Good level in a position description. Therefore, interview questions should also be scored at the Meets/Good level. It is important to be mindful that your interview questions relate back to the position description. If they don't, then you have to ask yourself why you are asking the question. If you've done your due diligence in the selection process, most of your candidates will likely fall into the Meets category. The great part about this piece is that each interviewer will be reviewing the candidate's responses by having the same working definition for each area upon which to score.

On the last page of the interview questions, provide a place for all of the scores to be added and a place to mark whether the scorer recommends, recommends with reservation or does not recommend the candidate.

Other Items to Consider from the Candidate

I mentioned earlier that our office has requested an Advising Philosophy from candidates in addition to their cover letter and resumé. This has made all the difference in the world to our process and is an appropriate request given that this is a part of our daily conversations. Consider what you could be asking of your candidates to help you determine who are the best ones to interview and eventually hire. Would you like the candidate to submit a sample of their work as a part of the application process? Perhaps you would like them to bring a work portfolio with them to the interview. Do you want them to do a short presentation or teach the group something? If so, what is the outcome your desire? What knowledge, skills and abilities are you expecting to see? What does "Exceed Expectations" look like in any of these examples?

Soliciting Feedback

Both the search committee and the staff committee, if you have one, should be provided an opportunity to submit their feedback, including total scores, each candidate's strengths, their areas for development, and any other comments they have as an interviewer they want to make known. This can be done through submitting their paper interview materials, an online survey tool or perhaps a survey function available to you through your workplace. Compile all the data and provide it to your search committee for review. Make sure you understand what the role of the Search Committee is in this process. Are they a deciding body or are they making a recommendation to you as the leader and decision maker or to someone else? Also, how long are you expected to keep interview materials after someone is seated in the position? Check with your Human Resources office. It may be several years.

As you read this, you may be thinking your staff may be resistant to change their hiring practices. Perhaps you do not need a major overhaul and just need to make a few tweaks instead. Consider if your current process works for you and is effective. What is your turnover? How long has your longest employee been there? How short? As Dave Ramsay says, "people don't mind change, they mind the way they're made to change." Involve them in the process and equip them to learn how to do the process and grow from it themselves.

Reference Checks

Do not skip this important step. I think many managers find this a futile effort because most people only ask others to be a reference that will speak favorably of them, which of course makes sense. These days I often get reference checks that have been emailed to me with a request to type my responses and return. I have never been a fan of this practice for two reasons: 1) I do not get a chance to talk with the person requesting the information. Sometimes the conversations that ensue during a reference check offer additional information and 2) all of the work is on me. It just doesn't seem right. There are many online resources with examples of solid reference check questions, and I have put my favorites on my website.

I strongly recommend that you ALWAYS speak with someone who has supervised this person, even if they're not on the candidate's reference list. You may want to consider telling potential candidates they must include a current or past supervisor on their reference list. You also want to ask some basic questions like their work attendance, work ethic, ability to follow through, and professional workplace behavior. You also want to ask questions about the candidate's areas for growth and development. Ask for an example of a time the reference provided feedback to the candidate and how it was received. Discuss challenges in the workplace, if any. Two of my favorite reference questions are: "Would you re-hire this person, if they are eligible to be rehired, why or why not?" This may seem like an uninformative question, but it is critical. I have worked with people over my career that were awesome at their job but wreaked havoc on the office by creating drama or stirring the pot of people's discontent. I would not rehire those individuals. Similarly, sometimes candidates were excellent in their previous position; but because of human relations related matters that caused their separation, a candidate is no longer eligible to return to their previous place of employment. This, of course, does not mean you should not hire them, but the matter may require further probing and a consultation with your own human resources department before proceeding further. My second favorite question is, "What could I do as this person's supervisor to support them in their role?" Because your role as a leader is to develop people, it is important to know on the front end what you need to pay attention to so you can be mindful of what a new employee may need from you as a supervisor.

When crafting your reference check questions, keep your organizational values in mind and think about questions that connect to the culture of your office or department. Regardless of whether or not you use questions that have been prepared for you, ones you have found online, or you are starting from ground zero, be intentional in your question selection. And remember, reference checks would not be a part the hiring practice if they were not important.

How to Make THE Decision

Bruna Martinuzzi, author of *The Leader as a Mensch: Become the Kind of Person Others Want to Follow* says, "Hire people who are smarter than you are—whose talents surpass yours—and give them opportunities for growth. It's the smart thing to do and it is a sign of high personal humility."

When it is time to decide who to hire, there are many factors in this decision. This begins with the candidate's application materials, their interview, their supporting materials, if any, their presentation/teach time, and feedback from your committee or other staff, if requested.

You must consider the facts at hand. Have your questions adequately and thoroughly given you the necessary information to make a strong hire? Does this person bring a necessary or missing skillset to the table? Do you have more than one equally qualified candidates but only one vacancy? Listen to your inner voice. You must not hire someone *solely* based on a feeling. Of course, you should like the person, but feelings change all the time and laying a foundation for your workforce on your good feelings about a candidate is like trying to build a castle on quicksand. Conversely, if you have a sixth sense about a candidate, investigate it. Do not brush it under the carpet. You have to discern if the candidate has a passion for the work or are they simply able to do the work. I have had this sixth sense feeling from time to time over the years and I ignored it. I had no plausible reason not to hire this person based on their skills and certainly could not justify to human resources why I did not want to hire a particular candidate. In those few cases, I ended up onboarding someone who ultimately was not happy, and they blamed me for it. They likely made the people around them unhappy too. Learn from the wisdom of my mistakes.

STRATEGY TIME:

1. Take the time to work with your staff to identify competencies/values you're seeking from candidates.
2. Take the time to train your team on BBI techniques and the candidate selection processes. If you think you do not have the time to do this and all you need is a warm body to fill the position, consider how much time you'll spend managing a person that is just warming their seat. Is that is how you want to spend your time?
3. Meet each interview candidate yourself using your own question set. I have used Patrick Lecioni's Hungry/Humble/Smart questions from his book *The Ideal Team Player* as a guideline. Also consider the questions the candidate asks you. A red flag is if they have no questions for you as the defined leader or just a question about the search process.

ACTION PLAN:

- In the next five days, I will:

_____

_____

_____

_____

_____

_____

- In the next 10 days, I will:

_____

_____

_____

_____

_____

_____

Needle in a Haystack

- In the next 30 days, I will:

___

___

___

___

___

___

___

- The person/people I need to talk to about this are:

___

___

___

___

___

___

___

CHAPTER 7

Do Not Pass GO

"The only thing worse than training your employees and having them leave is not training them and having them stay."
– Henry Ford

Your successful onboarding and training experience for new team members sets the tone for the rest of their experience and in many cases, yours as well. The formal onboarding process is more than showing your new staff member their office and handing them a set of keys. Just like we discussed in developing your office's culture, you must be intentional. You want to ensure that your new employee not only feels welcome and has the supplies they need, but also has a firm foundation for their first few days on the job. Regardless of your industry, the first person any new person should meet is their leader. During this meeting you are not just teaching your new hire the in's and out's of the organization and giving them their business cards, but more importantly, you are setting the tone for their experience. You are teaching the mission and vision and discussing your established team values. You are offering context of how your department or business functions within the larger context of the organization or industry. You want to communicate how their role fits into the puzzle. This is also a time for you to discuss your department's policies and procedures. Things like the hours of operation, when and how they get paid, what to do if they get sick or are running late and where the restroom and the photocopier are located are important for them to know. I like to think about it as a new employee's hierarchy of needs. They need the basics so they can build upon that as they complete their training.

Many organizations like to set personal performance goals with new employees within the first week of their onboarding, but I am not a fan of this. There simply is too much for a new person to learn in the first weeks of employment. The goal at this point is to equip the person to be successful from day one. They will have completed their HR paperwork and are excited to get started and contribute. Be sure to introduce them to others in the office. Depending on the size of your organization, I recommend taking the time the very first day to introduce your new person to others on the team. You can start with basic introductions: who is who and their role, how long they've been with the team and any points of connection you may be aware of (this could be that they're from the same state, attended the same college, have similar interests, etc.). Lastly, this is when you share your goals for the individual. For me, my goal for them is that they learn their job and understand their role. Depending on the nature and cycle of your department's work, this could take up to a year. That does not mean that the new team member is off the hook for developing professional goals, but I think any sooner than the three-month mark may be too soon.

For most new employees, the 'honeymoon high' ends around day 90 of employment. At this point, they have met their new colleagues, had a tour of the facility, know the rhythm of the department and have seen it in action. They have witnessed times of stress and leadership decision making and attended a staff meeting. The honeymoon is officially over and the reality of their situation has set in. As the leader, you have complete control over how long the honeymoon lasts with your onboarding and training experience. As with everything we have discussed thus far, this too must be intentional.

Now that your new person has had an initial onboarding experience, then you can get to the business of training. You want to build this with the end in mind. When professional NHL legend, Wayne Gretzky, retired he was asked what made him such a great ice hockey player and he said he was where the puck was going to be. In other words, he anticipated where the puck would go, and he went there. Approach your training practices the same way. What are the outcomes you have for their training experience? What do you want your new employee to be able to do, know and understand? If you weren't trained for your formal role as leader, imagine how someone with less knowledge or experience than you may feel and experience if they aren't trained properly (or at all) for their role. How can you expect them to perform well and be successful and reach your expectations for them? Award winning customer service speaker and author, Shep Hyken says, "Training helps teach the vision and mission, but employees must put the training into action to have meaning."

I love the television program *Undercover Boss*. This show has a CEO, or some similar upper-management leader go 'under cover' in their company interacting with different employees within the organization by posing as a reality television competitor who is learning the business as an entry-level employee. Because many of these leaders are often recognizable by their employees, they work with professional disguise artists to change their hair style, clothing, make-up, etc. so they become unrecognizable to those who may know them otherwise. It really is quite the transformation. They are then inserted into various locations within their multi-site organization and interact with their employees at all levels of it.

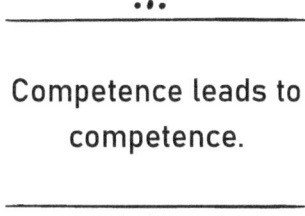

Competence leads to competence.

I love this show for many reasons. These leaders are people that care about their organization and understand that if they were not in disguise, they likely would not get the feedback they need to make their business better, simply because they are 'the boss.' The wonderful thing about this show is that not only are the employees they interact with changed and the business processes changed because of their feedback, but the leader is also profoundly and unexpectedly impacted. However, one of the things that always blows my mind is that these 'new employees' show up for a one-day experience and presumably within minutes they are operating the cash register or a forklift or interacting with customers. One episode I watched featured a massage therapy business CEO. Thirty minutes into the show, the trainer had this CEO giving a massage to a customer! It was mortifying to the undercover boss, who had never given a massage in her life before. I would imagine it may have been unnerving for the customer as well. Talk about jumping into the deep end. I realize that many of these crash course trainings may be for dramatic effect. Each episode of the show is only an hour after all. This leader is only there for one day, but the crash course 'training' often leaves the leader feeling flustered and looking like a ninny. This is not what you want for your new employee. Your work is too important to be left to a crash course. No matter how busy you may get, make sure it happens and happens well.

This chapter will discuss the value of onboarding and training your newest team members. Training does not have to be complicated or time consuming, it just has to be intentional and systematic. If you do not have the time, delegate the development of your training program to your leadership team or create a committee to develop the process. At the end of the day, all employees should have a similar onboarding experience, but the training itself needs to be customized at some level to each new person. Depending on the skill sets the new employee brings to the table, you may or may not need to cover certain parts of your training. However, with each piece of the training experience, you need to assess the measures you have put in place to ensure that the person is competent in that area. Remember, competence leads to confidence. The more competent the new employee becomes, the more confident they feel in completing their job duties. The more competent the new employee becomes, the more confident you become in their abilities and you can change gears in how you lead this person (remember, Situational Leadership!)

Because one of your jobs as a leader is to develop your employees, having them participate in the training process is a great way to help them also teach the values of your department as well as the mechanics of the job duties. When you are building your training program, start with the outcomes you have in mind and then think about the members of your team who can help build that component. Perhaps they have a particular passion for this part of their work? Maybe they are excellent at a specific skill or task? Who has an uncanny way of doing something or delivering a message? Even the least seasoned person has something to offer the next new person. How can you employ the expertise you have in your midst to develop a training program if you do not already have one? If you have one in place, how do you employ the expertise of the people in your midst to deliver your content?

One great way to ensure a successful training experience is to establish a new employee mentor program. This can be as formal or informal as you like and depends on your organization and the nature of your work. Regardless of the size or scope of what your business offers, a mentoring program is a great way to have ongoing training and provide a supportive, go-to person for your new employee. It is hard to anticipate every question a new person may have, and you may not be available to answer them all. Again, you do not want to leave things to chance. By providing a mentor to your new employee with the expectation for the mentor in place, the process can benefit both the more seasoned employee as well as your new person. I recommend that the mentor meet with his or her mentee at least once a week for at least a half hour, if not longer. These regular meetings are an opportunity for a weekly check-in. How are things going so far? What questions do you have? What do you need to know or understand? A component of this process is to ensure that whomever you identify to be a mentor is comfortable in doing so and is clear on the expectations you have for the process. I recommend that you put your mentor process in writing and provide a copy of it to your mentors, reviewing it as often as necessary, for quality control and to make changes to it based on the mentors' feedback. You may be wondering how to identify who your mentors should be. When you think about your workforce, ask yourself: Who are some of your most seasoned people doing the same work and doing it really well? Who are the top performers? Who consistently has performance reviews in which the employee goes above and beyond the call of duty? These are the people you want mentoring your newest folks. However, you have to be mindful to avoid consistently relying on your top performing staff members as they can become candidates for burnout. Also consider, who are your rising stars? Who, with the appropriate amount of support (remember Situational Leadership), can be challenged to grow by serving as a mentor to a new staff member?

Another component of a great training schedule is to provide a regular shadowing experience. I would recommend that your new employee begin by shadowing his or her mentor. This helps continue to build the trust-based relationship they have begun to establish. However, do not exclude others in the department from being given the opportunity to be shadowed as well. This is their opportunity to shine. If you have done a great job of recruiting, hiring and training your people, you can rest easy in this process. Depending on the job duties, your new team member may need to at least meet with if not also shadow others in a similar role within the organization.

The beautiful thing about a shadowing experience is that it provides your new team member the opportunity to see how the same job can be done in different ways. Each person can exemplify how they accomplish the mission and vision of your organization in their own unique way and using their own personal flair and style. This is an encouragement to the new person that they too will develop their own unique style as they become more comfortable in the role.

At some point during or after the training process, give your new person the opportunity to fly solo. When this will happen is dependent upon their role, their job duties, their previous experience, and how they have progressed and performed throughout the training process. Regardless of when you decide to let them 'loose,' you need to confirm that the person has met your training outcomes. This can be completed in a variety of ways, including but not limited to a personal one-on-one meeting with them to have them tell you what they know about the key areas of responsibility, witness them performing the task, or taking a quiz or test related to content area. Even when the person is successful in completing the assessments you have presented to them, it remains important that they are shadowed themselves, starting with the mentor. Depending on the variety of duties and tasks at hand, the mentor can shadow his or her mentee as much or as little as you think is pertinent to the new team member's growth and development, but I think at least two or three shadow experiences would be a good place to start and add on from there as necessary. As a part of the shadowing experience, time needs to be built in for both the mentor and mentee to meet beforehand for any remaining preparation and to answer final questions and again afterwards to debrief the experience.

As a side note, be sure you as the leader are aware of any HR practices that you need to know as it relates to new employees. Some new employees may be considered probationary. The probation period may be as few as three months and could be as long as 12 months. Either way, get clear on what probation means exactly. Does this mean that you can dismiss the person without cause during that probationary period? Does that mean that they do not receive certain employment benefits until the probationary period is over? Once you know, make a commitment to tell the new person what it means. Some HR on-boarding processes are better than others and you want to make sure your new staff member is also clear. If the probationary period is related to a possible dismissal at the end of the probationary period, this then means that once that period has passed, the rules on how you dismiss someone from their role changes, and you need to know and understand the process.

If you already have a training program in place, take the time to evaluate what you have already. Seek feedback from your current staff about improvements that could be made. What worked? What didn't? You could consider a focus group, identifying a training committee or offer an anonymous survey. This feedback can offer you concrete examples and ideas for improvement instead of relying on anecdotal evidence. Consider whether or not you are you satisfied with what it offers new employees? Is it specific to your department? Is it enough? After making necessary changes, implement them when you hire someone new. Once the training program is complete, seek feedback. This could be through one-on-one conversation, a focus group or an anonymous survey. Ask them about their experience and where improvements can be made. Our department experienced a massive exodus as a part of the 2021 'Great Resignation,' a phenomenon that occurred across the United States in which people voluntarily quit their jobs. Over the course of the next seven months, we worked to recruit, hire, onboard and train our new employees within a couple of weeks of each other. To make matters more complicated, the position that is responsible for training development was also vacant. The additional challenge is that we never had to employ the training program for so many people at one time. Given that we had turned over about half of our staff, we almost did not have enough seasoned staff members remaining to serve as mentors and the number of people that needed to shadow and be shadowed almost outweighed the talent I already had on hand. As of this writing, almost all of our new folks have completed the formalized training we have in place, but as our process changes in the coming months, there will be more training and shadowing that needs to be done. As we have been assessing their competencies in anticipation of flying solo soon, we are seeking feedback from them about how their experience could have been even better.

If you don't have any authority over the training program your organization offers, meet with your new employees anyway and seek feedback. Use that feedback to improve what you can in your department and share it with the appropriate people who can impact a change. In this way you are advocating for your future staff members either for your team or your organization. Either way, it is a win.

In 1965, Bruce Tuckman developed what he defined as the Stages of Group Development: Forming (group members finding their place, excited and anxious at the same time, need clarity on mission); Storming (the honeymoon is over and a person's personal nature surface, possibility for conflict to arise, may challenge the leader);

Norming (people know each other and are more appreciative of their colleagues' talents, have a greater commitment to goals, and are able to give thoughtful feedback); Performing (the team has gelled and is reaching its goals).[16] This is a continuum. As you onboard new team members, the group will naturally ebb and flow between each of these stages. As the leader, be mindful of what stage your team may be in at any given time as this impacts some of the decisions you will make about your training processes. (Tuckman later added a final stage, Adjourning, but it does not necessarily apply in a training setting).

If you do not have this already, include an outline or schedule for your onboarding and training program for each new staff member. Include what will happen on the first day, the first week and the first month. What are the objectives of each training session and the benchmarks for what each new employee should know or be able to do at the end of each phase of training? Then formalize how you will assess whether or not they are being met. For example, on the first day be sure that their office space has been cleaned and stocked with necessary supplies, business cards, business email or nametag (if appropriate). Any equipment in their area is operational and that a scheduled employee benefits session with the human resources department has already been set. Also include information about access keys, where the restroom and break room are located and where to park on a long-term basis. I also consider these things the hierarchy of needs for a new employee. In the first week, schedule a tour of the facility, introductions to colleagues or other key personnel if this didn't happen on the first day.

After all is said and done, training new people well is an issue of integrity. If you are haphazard in your onboarding and training, it is highly probable that their ability to perform to their potential is greatly reduced and therefore impacting your mission. As Brent Gleeson, former Navy SEAL and CEO of Taking Point Leadership says, "Ability + Motivation = Performance." The last thing you want to happen is to have your new team member go home at the end of their first day and tell their loved one that there is no formal training. Plus, evaluating your training can be a starting point on how to inform future trainings or professional development activities.

STRATEGY TIME:

1. Meet with your new staff members at the end of the 90-day period to seek feedback on their experiences so far and set interim personal performance goals.
2. Consider ways to include your current staff members in the on-boarding process whether that be formal or informal.
3. Establish metrics to confirm your new staff member is fully trained and has baseline competency before being formally placed into their role solo.

ACTION PLAN:

- In the next five days, I will:

_____
_____
_____
_____
_____
_____

- In the next 10 days, I will:

_____
_____
_____
_____
_____
_____

- In the next 30 days, I will:

- The person/people I need to talk to about this are:

CHAPTER 8

I Didn't Volunteer for This

"Employees cannot become more productive in every sense of the word unless they are provided with continuous on-the-job training."
– Gregory Balestrero, industrial engineer, CEO emeritus of Project Management Institute and author

Is your team equipped to be successful? This is a challenging question to ask yourself, especially if you have a broad range of employees. It is difficult to hit the bullseye when offering continued training or professional development. It is a delicate balance of offering titillating content and not boring the pants off the most seasoned people in the room. As you think about Tuckman's Stages of Group Development, where is your team? What can I do to equip my staff to be successful in their role and continue to build cohesiveness and a shared common vision? This is not an easy task. While many people are hungry and eager by nature or by virtue of being new, there are others that do not want to be developed because they are satisfied with where they are in their career or do not have a desire to grow in this way. They may have been in the role for many years, may be disengaged or personally distracted. Regardless of where your team members fall on this spectrum, your offering continued opportunities for your staff to grow in the role exemplifies your commitment to them. I think when times get super busy, it is easy to push these activities to the sidelines in exchange for more pressing matters. I know I have been guilty of this myself. However, this is also a delicate balancing act. You force people to participate and they feel resentful because they could or would be doing other things they see as more important. You push it until later and you could be accused of not offering a value added to the workplace. In order to make a good decision, you must keep your pulse on your people. It does not have to cost a lot of money or take a lot of time; it just has to be intentional. The more proactive you can be with your professional development activities, the more receptive folks will be. Whatever you decide to do, always connect it back to your mission.

For the most part, people desire growth and when you deny professional development opportunities, you open the door for a disengaged employee or their leaving. According to Legaljobs, "Out of 23 drivers of job satisfaction, survey participants ranked 'potential for growth' as the most important factor. This implies that organizations need to revisit the career development programs they offer and see if these are aligned with their employees' career satisfaction paths.[17]" Both disengagement and staff attrition are detrimental to your department's growth.

Staff members need different things from the team and have different reasons for wanting to meet. This chapter will address the value and importance of ongoing and consistent professional and staff development activities.

I have the letters A.C.T. on a sticky note attached to my computer desktop. This nugget is thanks to a *Minute with Maxwell* video I watched some years ago. The A stands for Apply to my life. C stands for Change. And T stands for Teach or Transfer to others. I think about this often when I learn new information. This is certainly true in the realm of professional development. In any activity you implement for your team, help them take A.C.T.ion on what they learned. This can be part of their personal professional goals or their professional development plan. As your team members become better professionals, everyone benefits. Therefore, make professional development a part of your workplace culture. Make it an expectation. Outside of professional conference attendance at the local, regional, national or international level that your industry may offer, which tend to get pricey, there are many examples of activities you can provide at low or no cost. I have tried all kinds of things over the years. You can read industry-related articles or book and discuss. You could bring in a content expert to present on a specific subject, or better yet look to your own ranks. Do you have anyone on staff that has a personal passion or specific knowledge about a subject that is relevant and pertinent to the team? Perhaps you are in an industry that is rapidly changing or has safety as a top priority in which ongoing training is essential to meet the mission of the organization. This may require weekly, monthly or quarterly briefings and updates.

Many years ago, I learned about a personality temperament assessment founded by Don Lowry entitled *True Colors®*. The assessment measures a variety of personality variables like communication and listening styles, values, learning styles among others and assigns one of four personality colors: Gold, Green, Orange, and Blue.[18] Golds tend to be your administrator types. Greens tend to be 'big picture.' Orange tend to be your bottom-line people and Blue tends to be more relationship oriented. Similar to other assessments like MBTI® and StrengthsFinder®, participants display personality characteristics from any of the four colors, but one is more dominant than others. There are many fascinating components to this assessment, but my takeaway as a leader was to A.C.T. on it by applying and introducing this to my staff meeting structure. The two key components that were added was at least one staff meeting per month dedicated to staff development, which were activities dedicated to people getting to know one another better, and at least one staff meeting per month dedicated to professional development, which were activities dedicated to people becoming better in their role. When you decide to implement something that will work for your workplace, you can assign a committee from your team to research and put together a proposal for activities.

The most meaningful professional development activities that landed the best with my team and worked well for me has come in the form of a series. One-off workshops are sometimes more appropriate when you need to invest more time and take a deep dive to develop the team, solve a problem, or plan for the future. However, identifying a topic at the beginning of every calendar year, fiscal year or even quarter has a lot of value. Let's assume you will dedicate two hours a month to this activity. You can decide as the leader what the topic needs to be, but you will get more buy in if you solicit ideas from your team. Your first meeting can lay out the schematics of the series and provide an initial big picture overview of the topic. This can be led by you or a member of your team. If you have a committee of folks who have identified a topic and planned the series, let them take the lead. This was the case in my office. We had a professional development committee and they decided our office needed to focus on the ethics involved in the day-to-day of our profession. They solicited ethical situations from the staff they had encountered in their daily work and converted them into case studies. The committee selected four or five of the most compelling that were submitted and as a staff we dissected the case studies and discussed how we will handle these situations in the future or put systems into place to mitigate them from happening again. From this meeting, the team decided we need to have a Statement of Ethics, which we would publish on our departmental website. The next monthly meeting, we brainstormed ideas on what needed to be included in our statement and developed a Statement that is still used today. Our final coup de gras event was a panel discussion with other professionals from our larger industry, which represented a variety of points of view. We revisited the case studies once again and added their points of view on the issues on the table. By far, this was the most meaningful and purposeful we had ever offered up to that point. Because of our work cycle, we realistically can only have four or five formal professional development workshops per year. However, because the series was well received and meaningful, we have continued to offer professional development in this format.

Keep in mind that not all development activities have to be about work. You spend more waking hours with your colleagues in some cases than you do your own family members, so take the time to build a community at work. You also want to spend some of your team time in staff development activities. However, staff development is more about developing relationships between colleagues through a shared experience. This can be through celebrations such as birthdays, weddings, graduations and babies. They can also be through field trips to nearby exhibits or museums. You could go on a walking tour around the facilities, the town, or city in which your organization is located. You could volunteer at your local food pantry or Habitat for Humanity group. If you have a staff member that has a non-profit that is near and dear to their heart, ask them how your office could get plugged in. Our office has done all kinds of fun and interesting things. These informal and fun events allow people to relax and enjoy one another and most of them are low or no cost.

> **Remember that people tune into the radio station in their head WIIFM (What's In It For Me)**

I realize that not all office settings allow for an extended time away from the office for a field trip, so instead you may have to get even more creative and use formalized break or lunch times for a quick and fun event, or use staff meeting time. As we have discussed, some people are more extroverted than others, so not every idea will appeal to all people. You may experience some initial resistance especially if this is a new endeavor. Remember that people tune into the radio station in their head WIIFM (What's In It For Me) and that each person has a unique set of needs from any time a group gets together for a meeting. Think about appealing to not only what each individual can get from a staff development activity, but also what they can contribute.

Sometimes, the least enthusiastic person can become enthusiastic if the topic is something they have interest in or are passionate about.

Cost is always on the mind of anyone who manages a budget. Some organizations value staff and professional development as a part of their identity and investment in their people and as a result, funding exists and is available to any staff member who is interested in accessing it. Sometimes this is not the case and funding is limited. If you have the ability to decide where your budget money goes, build in some funding for these events. If not, investigate internal or external grant funding or discuss with your next line supervisor. There may be funds more readily available at their discretion for this type of use.

STRATEGY TIME:

1. Assess where your people and team need to grow. Does your professional national/international organization have identified competencies? If not, create your own.
2. A.C.T. on what you've learned. Tell your team what you've learned and model the way. Start small. Always include the 'why'.
3. Create a Professional and Staff Development plan for your team. This could be through your Leadership Team or by committee and then implement it.
4. Strike a balance- too much can create burnout and resentment. Always consider timing.

I Didn't Volunteer for This

Now, write down what you have decided to do:

Act

_____

_____

_____

_____

_____

_____

_____

Change

_____

_____

_____

_____

_____

_____

_____

Leadership in the Trenches

Teach/Transfer

CHAPTER 9

I Did a Great Job, I Promise

"A performance appraisal that is conducted effectively leads to greater employee morale, higher productivity, creating a positive culture and improved overall performance and effectiveness of an organization."
– Kumar Parakala, President of GHD Digital

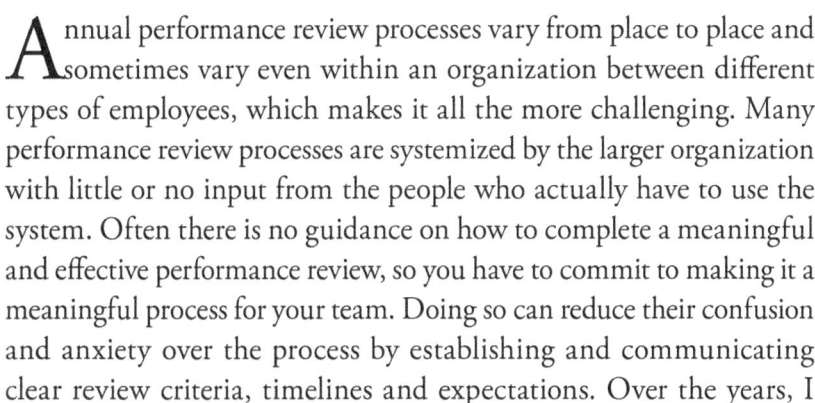

Annual performance review processes vary from place to place and sometimes vary even within an organization between different types of employees, which makes it all the more challenging. Many performance review processes are systemized by the larger organization with little or no input from the people who actually have to use the system. Often there is no guidance on how to complete a meaningful and effective performance review, so you have to commit to making it a meaningful process for your team. Doing so can reduce their confusion and anxiety over the process by establishing and communicating clear review criteria, timelines and expectations. Over the years, I have found a few ways to make the review process less painful for everyone involved.

More times than not a performance review is directly related to a salary increase, although this is not always the case. It really does depend on the larger organization. One place I worked granted systematic raises as long as you had a 'Successful' performance review and you were not currently on any kind of work improvement plan due to poor performance. Any merit-based raises, if and when any funding was available for them, came at the discretion of the department director. Other organizations require a rating of "Good" or "Successful" on a three or five-level scale in order to be eligible for a salary increase. Any additional merit funding is based on a higher than "Good" rating and sometimes at the discretion of the department's director and other times at the discretion of the next level supervisor or higher. In other places, there may be no performance review whatsoever so as long as you were in good standing (i.e. you weren't in trouble or causing any), you received a salary increase. This may be in a situation in which there is a union or a contract of some sort. As with all other processes, you should assume you will receive little or no guidance and must educate yourself on the process, the expectations, and any working definitions to effectively rate your team members within the related guidelines. Also, be sure to know when these reviews are expected to occur. Is it on the annual calendar, a fiscal year or something else? What is the difference, if any, for new employees? If it is different, how so and what are the expectations for that process?

As you might imagine or have experienced yourself, this process is wrought with anxiety and stress in many cases for all parties involved, especially if there is any potential for a salary increase. The research suggests that salary is not a primary motivator for employee engagement, but I have found so far that no one has ever told me, "Please, I enjoy my job so much, I do not want you to give me more money." It simply just does not happen.

Also make note of how the process works. In several places I have worked, the review consisted of an annual meeting with my supervisor, followed up with a letter on company letterhead that went into my employee file and documented what I had accomplished that year. Another place I worked had a web-based system in which employee goals were documented, and company values and job duties each got a rating ranging from Exceptional to Poor. This then went to the next line supervisor for review and approval and then once again to a supervisor after that. The process took months.

No matter how time consuming it is. No matter how poor the systems or processes you have to deal with may be, failing to complete the performance review process in your department will impact your employee morale in a big way and doing a slipshod job will damage your moral authority making it difficult for your team to trust you as their leader. Like many other things in leadership, this is an integrity issue.

This chapter will focus on the formal performance review process and offer some insight and lessons learned into how to make it a meaningful experience for both the giver and receiver.

When I first started being responsible for conducting performance reviews as the primary supervisor, I had several goals in mind:
1) Reduce stress and anxiety for my team about the process overall.
2) Complete all reviews on time or in advance of the larger organization's deadline.
3) Do a thorough and thoughtful job on each review.
4) Make sure I am consistently applying the criteria for all staff members in each review category.

I asked our HR department for a definition of the evaluation ratings. What I received was very vague and not helpful at all. I remember thinking how in the world am I going to do this? In fact, the very first time I had to do this process, I had just started my position and had to evaluate people I just met! Talk about crazy. Not only did I have to learn the system, but I also had to figure out how to fairly and equitably evaluate each member of a team that I had just met a couple of weeks prior. One of the first things I did as a part of my own onboarding experience was meet one-on-one with each team member to learn more about who they were, their goals and what they were currently working on. Once I realized there was no way around completing these evaluations because the default rating was automatically "Good" if they were not completed at all or by the deadline, which, by the way, is a TERRIBLE idea. I, nonetheless, pushed on. I asked each person to complete a self-evaluation and to highlight their key accomplishments in the process. I told them that this was a time to brag about themselves, even if it made them feel a little uncomfortable. In my short time there, I quickly surmised that this was a hard-working bunch and there was not a slacker among them. I decided at the time that everyone earned at least a "Good" rating, and a few earned higher ratings based on the documentation I had available to me about their performance prior to my arrival. I also made sure to make careful notes as I completed their evaluation that I was new to the role and had only known these individuals for a very short time. I met with each person on the team and reviewed the comments and ratings I had assigned to the various categories and made any updates or corrections in real time. Overall, it went pretty well given the circumstances, but I learned after the fact that this particular year there was some merit money but only staff members who had a rating greater than "Good" were eligible. Imagine my dismay when I learned this new information and how painful it was for me to tell the staff members who had *only* received an overall 'Good" rating would not be receiving any additional raise dollars that year. Tears flowed. Would I have scored anyone differently in light of that information? It is hard to say now, but it sure was a crappy way to start my tenure.

As I mentioned earlier, the performance review process is often fraught with anxiety for everyone involved. This is largely due to leaders not being taught how to effectively write a review or lead a review meeting. Because of that, sometimes employees arrive at their performance review only to be told that they have been doing something wrong throughout the entire review period and this is the first time they have heard about it. I had a colleague tell me one time that at her previous place of employment, during the review meeting with their supervisor, all employees were expected to come with two things they didn't like about their colleagues or something they knew they had done wrong. I had to pick my jaw up off the floor when she told me that. I cannot even imagine. How inappropriate. I have had an experience myself when I was surprised by unexpected comments from my supervisor made at my end of the year review. I vowed then and there that I would never surprise anyone at their performance review.

Others are anxious because they do not like talking about themselves or because their self-esteem has taken a hit somewhere along the way. So, my goal is to try to reduce any anxiety about the process. From the very beginning, starting Day One when I meet a new staff member, I explain the annual review process, give them a copy of what they will see in the online portal, the review timeline from the previous season, and the review criteria. I also tell them that there will be no surprises during this time. I will not be telling them for the first time that they are doing a good job and I will not be telling them for the first time that something is wrong.

Over the years I have tried different approaches with the self-evaluation. While it is always expected, I take their commentary about their performance to heart and do my best to fold it into the review itself. One year I attended a Supervisor Workshop in which we watched a video featuring the conductor of one of the major orchestras in the country. This conductor also taught graduate music courses at the nearby college. He told a story of how all of his graduate students were so focused on getting an "A" that they lost the joy in the learning and becoming better at their craft, so he told everyone at the beginning of the semester that everyone was getting an "A." They just had to keep it. This story got my wheels spinning and I thought to myself, "What if I tell my staff that everyone is getting an 'A' (or the highest review rating) on their performance review?" I thought that perhaps this would also help further reduce the anxiety and help put people at ease. I set myself a task to begin the self-evaluation process when they set their annual goals. This involved their writing a letter to their future selves. It must discuss what they had already accomplished and examples of how they accomplished it. At the end of the review period, they completed their self-evaluation through the online portal reflecting on whether or not they had actually achieved the goals they had set forth to complete. While the goals portion of the annual review never received a rating, it was a worthwhile exercise. I only did this for a couple of review cycles simply because it was not netting the results I had hoped for. Some staff members did a much better job than others in the process because some were more self-reflective or had better writing skills than others. I also did not have the time or know how to run a writing workshop. However, the problem remained with the ability to consistently apply annual review ratings in an equitable and fair way for each employee. The vague definitions HR had for each rating left the barn door so wide a small airplane could fly through it. Almost everything fit. It was difficult to be discerning.

As time has passed, I think I have found a way to work within the performance review system using the definitions provided to me by HR but drilling it down to what that looks like in our department. I did this because once the leadership team and new organizational structure I was aiming to put in place was implemented, I would have staff members that once reported to me reporting to someone else. It was important that not only was the criteria clear, but that it was also consistently applied. I wanted to make sure that everyone understood the purpose of the review process is to reflect on and discuss their accomplishments and contributions to the department based on their job descriptions, as well as develop an action plan for their future within the departmental goals.

From there, alongside my leadership team, I created a rubric with each of the performance review ratings on the left in a column and then in the right column I wrote the HR definition for that particular rating. Included below this were examples of what would be expected to be demonstrated by an employee in order to receive the rating they desired. So, in some ways, this employed the 'everyone gets an A' mindset but was in the past tense instead of in the future. All of this was captured in one document and also included the timeline for our departmental process completion within the deadlines established by the larger organization. The process to create this content took less than two hours and has saved me significant time later. Everyone received a copy in advance of the review period and each new employee that is onboarded also gets a copy, so no matter when a person begins their employment with us, they know what is expected.

Another thing that I have changed over the years involves when the team members receive a copy of their written review. In my earlier years, I would save the 'reveal' until they arrived at my office for their review meeting. I am sure this didn't help with the anxiety factor, but I told everyone in advance that the document wasn't finalized until the meeting was over and we could make any necessary changes as we went through each portion of the review. Overall, it wasn't terrible, but I did not love it either. During the same time, I was also participating in the review process as a person being reviewed. My supervisor always sent me a copy of my written review in advance of our meeting. It never dawned on me that I should do the same. I guess it did not occur to me because I tend not to be anxious about these types of meetings. Nevertheless, some years ago, I started to do the same and I do not think I will ever go back to doing something different. I tell everyone that they must complete their self-evaluation by a specified date so that I have time to review it and apply it to the comments I make myself in their review. Then I typically give the completed review to each staff member at least 24 hours, if not longer, before their review meeting with me. I ask them to read it and come prepared to discuss any discrepancies. By and large, the discrepancies tend to be spelling errors; but from time-to-time I may have forgotten that they were part of a major project or committee. For the most part I pride myself on paying attention to the great work my folks are doing and use this process as an opportunity to provide specific examples of it. So, to make it easier on yourself, either use whatever tools are in place with your current system or develop one yourself in which you can keep track of the key tasks, projects and accomplishments of your staff for this purpose. If your system is online and there is an opportunity to upload examples of their work, do it! Kathryn Minshew, founder and CEO of The Muse says, "Done right, a performance review is one of the best opportunities to encourage and support high performers and constructively improve your middle and lower-tier workers." If there are areas where someone wants to grow, then this can be a part of the goal-setting process for the next year.

Even if your organization does not have a formal review process or it is inconsistently applied, everyone deserves feedback — even if it is just once a year. Take the time to formally invest in your employees in this way. If you have a small organization in which you have daily contact with your team members and have regular one-on-one meetings about their performance, then perhaps a once-a-year sit-down is overkill, but if you don't do either, then think about how you can employ this strategy. In May 2019, Gallup wrote, "When managers provide weekly feedback, team members are 5.2x more likely to strongly agree that they receive meaningful feedback, 3.2x more likely to strongly agree they are motivated to do outstanding work, and 2.7 x more likely to be engaged at work."[19] Feedback is powerful. Similarly, you may find that you are in an organization in which there is no accountability above you and no negative consequences for you if you don't complete a formal evaluation. As I just said, everyone deserves feedback regardless of what people above or beside you do. And lastly, you may have had negative experiences yourself in the performance review process and this is sad; however, you are now in a position to effectively and positively impact the process for someone else. Do not let your personal traumatic experiences in this way cause you not to take great care when completing the performance review process for the people you serve. They deserve better. Just remember that most of us have never been taught how to do it and do it well.

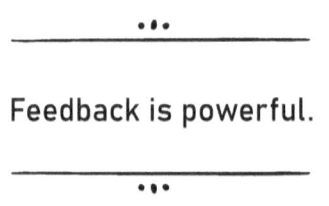

Feedback is powerful.

In effort to secure a more well-rounded assessment of your employee's overall job performance, consider seeking feedback from others in the department or organization that are not the employee's peers. To be clear, this is NOT an opportunity for others to evaluate. It is, however, an opportunity for you to collect additional information about an employee's performance. For example, does this person complete tasks on time when those tasks are connected to someone else's job duties? Does this person attend meetings you also do not attend as expected? Does this person contribute to project work? Does this person respond in a timely manner to verbal or written communication?

If you have employees participating in work groups or committees, you could ask work group leaders or committee chairs to complete a three-question survey or feedback form about how your employee performed within these groups. You do not want to bog down other busy people with complex metrics or feedback forms, so this could be accomplished quickly using a Likert scale and perhaps an opportunity for short comments, if appropriate.

STRATEGY TIME:

1. Be transparent with the process. Put the timeline and due dates, review criteria, self-evaluation deadlines, review expectations out there well in advance.
2. If you have an employee that is not performing up to minimum expectation standards, then tell them well in advance of the performance review process and give the individual an opportunity to improve. Agree upon specifically what needs to happen. You may need to get your HR Employee Relations person involved depending on the situation, so be sure to consult with them as appropriate.
3. Speak life into your people. Use the performance review time to set their personal performance goals that you and the individual agree upon together. Then meet consistently as appropriate.

ACTION PLAN:

- In the next five days, I will:

  _____

  _____

  _____

  _____

  _____

  _____

- In the next 10 days, I will:

  _____

  _____

  _____

  _____

  _____

  _____

I Did a Great Job, I Promise

- In the next 30 days, I will:

  _____

  _____

  _____

  _____

  _____

  _____

  _____

- The person/people I need to talk to about this are:

  _____

  _____

  _____

  _____

  _____

  _____

  _____

CHAPTER 10

Multi...what?

"Leaders who fail to embrace, manage and develop cohesive teams that thrive and succeed across generational differences will soon succumb to constant conflicts, silos, separatism, low morale, stagnate performance & inconsistent productivity."
– Ty Howard, former professional football player and motivational speaker

I grew up without the internet. Shocking, right?! Both of my parents worked outside the home once I started school so therefore, I was a latch key kid and learned to be independent and self-reliant from a very early age. I used the now extinct Dewey Decimal system to look up a book in the library. I grew up with a set of Encyclopedia Britannica in the family room. Our one family telephone in the kitchen was attached to the wall with a long cord to move into the next room if you wanted privacy for your call. I remember saving up enough money as a teenager to buy a telephone to put in my bedroom and thought that was something else. Now I carry a phone in my pocketbook. My first computer was a Tandy system from Radio Shack that I took to college my freshman year in the footlocker my father used when he was in the military. My 18" screen color television with a dial to change the channel was my monitor. I sent my first email in 1993 in my first professional job on a computer that had a bright blue background with white letters that blinked as I typed them. Now, I spend a significant part of my day managing an email account with thousands of emails and folders and flags and reminders.

When I first started my professional life, I was only a few years older than the oldest person on my team. There really was not much of a generational divide. However, as I have continued to work and have gotten older, I have had the opportunity throughout my career to work with people from all walks of life, races, ethnicities, and belief systems and have traveled to other states and countries. Diversity abounds. Unfortunately, today's diversity discussion has created societal division instead of cohesion driven by politics, popular culture and media commentary. However, I believe the true definition of diversity is a celebration in humanity.

The one area that is often left out of the diversity conversation is the impact of generational diversity on the workers themselves. Each person has been influenced by historical events like war, social movements, the AIDS epidemic, energy crises, school and church shootings, the economy and who is seated as President in the White House or other global leaders. We all bring the impact of these experiences to work with us every day regardless of whether or not we are conscious of it. Those experiences create one of many filters in which we view the world and our work.

Generational influences + childhood lessons + life experiences + workplace expectations = perceptions of reality

Generational influences + childhood lessons + life experiences + workplace expectations = perceptions of reality.

As leaders, we need to be mindful of the generational influences because it is possible to have 4-5 generations in the same work group at any one time. According to a LinkedIn article, the global labor force participation for workers aged 20-65 in 2020 will find workplaces staffed by 43.1% who will be Millennials and 20.7% will be Gen Z. By 2030, the combined group will be 74.4%, but then an entirely new generational group will be entering the workforce.[20] It is essential we know and seek to understand the characteristics of these generations. Not only will you be able to become a more effective leader, but you will also be able to make better decisions. Because of generational differences, you can potentially mitigate conflict and work to maximize the strengths of your team members.

This chapter will touch on the different generations that are in the workplace today and how leaders can maximize this diversity for the health of an organization. The table below outlines some key characteristics from each generation based on the research I have done on this topic or workshops I have attended. The list of characteristics could be expanded to be much longer as there is prolific information about each of these groups available; however, I chose to highlight particular characteristics that may be important to note when thinking about workplace culture, programmatic efforts and the needs of your individual team members.

Leadership in the Trenches

Name	Birth Year	Characteristics	Possible Conflict
Traditionalists	1922-46	Work is a privilege Disciplines and value a self-denial work ethic Conform to traditional roles and hierarchies	Likely either deceased or no longer in the workplace.
Baby Boomers 71.6 million in the US	1947-64	Strong work ethic motivated by wealth, rank, prestige Team players who do not go against peers Question authority but desire to hold higher ranks Believe in growth and expansion	Baby Boomers see Millennials and Generation X as lacking discipline and focus.
Gen X 65.2 million in the U.S.	1965-77/80	Experienced independence Thrive on change Independent, flexible, adaptable Casual approach to authority Nontraditional orientation about time and space Value flexibility and risk-taking; change is normal and desirable Loyalty is situational Relatively tech savvy/digital immigrant	Generation X sees Baby Boomers as resistant to change, dogmatic in their thinking, sexist, defensive and lacking in creativity. They also see Millennials as arrogant.

Multi...what?

Name	Birth Year	Characteristics	Possible Conflict
Gen Y/ Millennials 72.1 million in the U.S.	1978-94 or 1995/96 depending on the source	Shapes how they search for information, solve problems and communicate Most educated, most diverse Crave constant feedback and praise Top priority is stability Hard workers, good students Everybody works together to achieve goals Hates conflict, consensus builders Excited about working in teams Most important in the workplace is getting along with a widely diverse group Place high value on helping others Tech savvy Accustomed to structuring time, working from schedules and following rules	Millennials see Generation X as having poor problem-solving skills and being slow to respond. They also see Baby Boomers as resistant to change, dogmatic in their thinking, sexist, defensive, and lacking in creativity.

Leadership in the Trenches

Name	Birth Year	Characteristics	Possible Conflict
Gen Z Nearly 68 million in the U.S.	1995-1997, depending on the source -2010-2012.	Entrepreneurial Do not prefer project work Competitive Likes to work independently; judged by their own merits rather than the merits of their team Don't want to rely on others to get work [projects] done Willing to work hard [to achieve dreams] but expect rewards Seek advancement in the workplace Many skipping higher ed to enter workforce (avoid debt) Do not have harsh lines between work and home life Expect to be catered to Lower attention spans than previous generation Overly reliant on devices	Youngest at age 18 would have entered the workforce in 2013.

Multi...what?

Name	Birth Year	Characteristics	Possible Conflict
Gen A (Alpha) ~48 million in the U.S.	2010/12-2025 Children of the Millennials	Likely an only child Greater chance of growing up selfish Expecting instant gratification Prefer communication through images and voice in lieu of typing or texting	Oldest of this generation will turn 18 in 2028.

See references for sources used to create this table

As a Gen Xer, extrovert and auditory learner, I prefer talking problems out and seeking input from others for solutions. You already know that I am not a digital native. My general philosophy is that I just simply want the machine to work. I do not want to understand the how or why it works. Because of this, when I do not know how to use a part of a software program, my first reaction is to go talk to someone about it. Occasionally, I will pluck around the various options at the top of the screen to try to find what I'm looking for, but I often find that inefficient and time consuming, so my usual tendency is to seek out someone else who is more knowledgeable. Several years ago, this 'someone' was my office manager, who was many years my junior, a member of Generation Y. From my perception she was very tech savvy. After all, her job required her to have technology skills and she often created short videos to explain our appointment management software to other people who were starting to use the product.

I remember beelining it to her office one morning because I could not figure out how to get the software program I was using to do what I needed it to do. When I presented my problem to her, she responded, "I don't know either. Let's Google it." Well, duh. I can do THAT. So, while she still helped me find the answer I was seeking, I sulked back to my office afterwards berating myself for bothering her with something I was quite capable of doing myself. I tell this story to illustrate a clear example of generational diversity in action. Because I didn't grow up with the internet, I just do not think of it as a go-to source. Remember, I had encyclopedias as my reference growing up. So, in the future, every time I felt the urge to go ask her how to do something, especially as it related to technology, I would go to YouTube first in a good faith effort to find a video that would show me how to do it. Most of the time I was successful.

Another generational observation I have made, especially since having my own children start to interact with technology, is that many Gen Z and presumably future Gen A people do not use their smart phones to call others. In fact, I have found that many are phone averse. That concept is so foreign to me. Isn't that what a phone is for….to call people? I had another Gen Y colleague who was extremely tech savvy. She ordered all of her groceries online, all of her take out lunches via an app on her phone and she never solved a problem she had with a company by using the phone. She always used the company's website chat function. This also seemed much more time consuming and inefficient than picking up the phone to call and speak with someone. She was a strong advocate for any chat feature offered for any question she had. I decided to give this a whirl when I was attempting to solve a problem after I discovered I made an error on an online order I made just minutes before. I'll spare you the gory and sorted details, but I ended up spending way too much time 'chatting' with the customer service representative in an effort to try to resolve the issue. I ultimately still ended up picking up the phone and calling the company so that I could speak with someone. I had to chuckle to myself. I did give it the ole college try, but I think I'll stick to using the phone in the future.

I mention these examples not only because when I look back at those situations, I have to laugh at myself, but because I also want to illustrate a point that your team members are all going to approach their daily tasks in different ways because of not only who they are and their strengths, but also because of their generational approaches to problem solving, their attitudes about work, their relationship with technology and their perceptions of reality. Give people the space, latitude and grace to do their work. If you have a staff member who is struggling with learning something new or employing the technology at hand, ask them what they need to learn. It may be a book. It may be a person. Or it may be leaving them to their own efforts and finding a YouTube video. The end result is still the same.

You also need to think about your customers. How can your services meet their needs and keep the lines of communication coming? If your phone isn't ringing, it may not mean that they do not have questions or want your services, but what generational mechanisms are you employing to get your messages to them. Do you have social media accounts? Do you use email and texting? Do you have a texting or chat service? You may not want to be the one managing them and some of these may not even be on your radar because you are not familiar with them, but undoubtedly you have someone on your team who would love to contribute or oversee your efforts in this area. Employ their expertise.

We discussed the StrengthsFinder® in an earlier chapter and this is another area where you can consider the innate talents of your team and think about how their generational influences can strengthen the goals of your department. One of the things that makes a great team is that each person's strengths are 'sharpening the edges' of their colleagues' strengths. I love that. As a leader, you have to be willing to learn about and understand the generations from which they come and approach your learning from a place of humility. What kind of leader do you need to be for each of your team members? How can you use what you know about their generation to manage expectations or improve your communication? Is there a way you can better approach their personal professional goals in the season of life they are in? What skills might each one of them want to learn and how can you make it so based on their learning preferences?

We all have a lot to learn from each other. Think of yourself as a great conductor of a marvellous symphony. Each instrument has its own unique contribution to the sound the group produces. The same is true of the people on your team.

STRATEGY TIME:

1. Learn about the generations of your people. This helps with problem solving and communication. It also lends to greater compassion as a leader.
2. Use strengths as a platform for celebration. Put diverse groups of people together (age, race, gender, ability) on work teams, small groups, or committees.
3. Make plans with your team and customers with generational diversity in mind. Each person has value. Each person has a role.

Multi...what?

ACTION PLAN:

- In the next five days, I will:

_____

_____

_____

_____

_____

_____

- In the next 10 days, I will:

_____

_____

_____

_____

_____

_____

- In the next 30 days, I will:

- The person/people I need to talk to about this are:

CHAPTER 11

People Are Who They Are

"Joy has little to do with what's happening to you but more to do with what's happening inside of you." – Pastor Skip Heitzig

Emotions can make bad leaders. Why? Because they are like waves in the ocean and change all of the time. The interesting thing about waves is that what they are really transmitting is energy, not water. If we think about our emotions as energy as well, it is easy to see why we should not lead with our emotions. For example, take a storm surge, a long wave triggered by high winds and continual low pressure or a tsunami, which occurs when water is suddenly displaced due to submarine earthquakes, volcanoes or landslides. Both of these happen very quickly moving massive amounts of water and widespread destruction. On the other hand, consider a hurricane, which is often slow moving and can sustain high velocity high winds and can cover both land and sea for days, also causing massive destruction. Someone who always operates from a place of strong emotion can change the temperature in your office within hours (tsunami) or days (hurricane). As a leader, you want to be a surface wave, consistent, reliable, slow and steady. This way you are prepared to handle the tsunamis and hurricanes that come your way.

Rewind your day and remember all the emotions you experienced even before your workday began…the alarm clock sounded, the snooze button pressed, your partner snored, the kids sang, the dog begged, breakfast happened (or not), the commute stalled, you searched for a parking spot…you name it. Now stop and take a moment to recount your morning. How many emotions did you experience in your first hours of the day? And you haven't even walked into the front door of your office building. Now consider that every person you work with also had their own set of emotions this morning. It's a wonder we all make it to work every day!

> You can take the temperature of your team at any time, but you control the thermostat of your office

While it may never be explicitly stated in your position description or job duties, part of your job as a leader is to manage emotions. In fact, you can take the temperature of your team at any time, but you control the thermostat of your office. If you panic, they will panic. If you're stressed, then they will be stressed. Keeping the emotional thermostat of your office at a consistent level is important. An example I can offer is a story a colleague told me several years ago of a time when her supervisor had brought a variety of bagged chips and other snack items to a staff meeting offering them to her team as a treat. What she failed to remember is the members of her team had made a commitment to have a healthier lifestyle and as a result chose not to eat any of her offerings. A short time into the meeting, the supervisor shouted at the group for their ungratefulness and started shoving potato chips into her mouth. True story. Tsunami. Hopefully, she was just having a bad day; but if her behavior was consistently like this, then over time she was damaging her moral authority. Hurricane. John Maxwell says that questions are the key that unlocks the door to connection. Had she chosen to respond by asking a question or two, perhaps this scenario wouldn't have unfolded as it did. People may be able to forgive a tsunami if the leader has some humility, but people leave organizations because of hurricane leaders.

Now, I have definitely had my bad days, but I generally work to keep my attitude positive and my emotions even. I have never shouted at anyone, pouted, or had a temper tantrum even when there were times I would have loved to have done any of those things. However, I have had members of my staff shout at me, pout, have temper tantrums, give me ultimatums and send emails so horrific that I sat in my office and cried after reading them. One time I had a staff member so mad at me for a decision I made she did not agree with that she would barely speak to me for a couple of days. When I finally got her to give voice to her unusual distance and silence, she let her feelings fly. Her words spewed all over me like puss from a giant pimple. It flattened me. It took the entire weekend for me to recover. People can be mean, but one of the things I have learned is that the way people treat us is more often a reflection of the relationship they have with themselves than anything it has to do with you. Let that sink in.

Don't Expect Apologies

I have learned not to expect apologies for bad behavior. And this is just something you too may have to come to terms with. People who shout and pout and have tantrums are troubled by something far deeper than the interaction you are having. You may have no idea what it is about, and it is possible your interaction was the unfortunate catalyst for the outburst. I am a firm believer in you reap what you sow and sometimes saying nothing is saying everything, so pick your battles. However, do not excuse it. Depending on the situation, disciplinary action may be necessary, so do not be tempted to sweep bad behavior under the carpet. I have definitely done this and as Andy Stanley says in his book *Principle of the Path*, "What you resist will persist." There have been times I have extended grace just a little too far and it has not served me or my team well.

On a positive note, I have also had staff members come to my office in tears because of devastating personal news, to share exciting news about something happening in their lives, or to ask for prayer.

Managing Expectations

Because one of the unwritten rules of being a leader is managing emotions, you cannot escape it. However, you are not responsible for feeling the feelings with them. And you are not responsible for counseling your staff through their emotions. But I do think you are expected to be there for them. You should also be prepared to refer them to services or resources available through their employment such as an employee assistance program. You just have to know your limits in any given emotionally charged situation so you can best serve the person in front of you. If you take the time to manage expectations, you can manage emotions, which will result in better managing conflict and getting to the truth.

Part of managing emotions is managing expectations. That includes their expectations for the limits of what you can and will do for them and where your level of authority begins and ends within the larger organization. I tend to share as much information as I am able and seek input from my team on processes that directly impact them. Simon Sinek says, "More information is always better than less. When people know the reason things are happening, even if it's bad news, they can adjust their expectations and react accordingly. Keeping people in the dark only serves to stir negative emotions."

This is a tough chapter. Humans are complex and much of your daily work will be helping people manage their emotions. This is why communication is so important…not just the why, but your care for others in your charge. The challenge is that many don't realize you too have your own emotions to manage. This is one of the reasons why leadership can be lonely. Who can you talk to when you have a bad day? People are selfish and sometimes others are so wrapped up in their own emotions that they often don't think that you have emotions too.

Empathy versus Compassion

Empathy and compassion make good bed fellows. Both are important. They are closely linked, and, in some cases, they are interchangeable depending on the situation. In the current times, there is a lot swirling on social media about empathy. What it is and what it looks like. I think the true definition of empathy has gotten lost somewhere along the way. Empathy is broad and how people employ and respond to it depends on each individual. Some people define empathy as feeling the emotions *with* the person. Others define it as recognizing the feelings of another person and trying to put yourself in their shoes. I have struggled with both of these definitions.

By and large, I have low empathy. In fact, it is number 33 on my list of 34 on the CliftonStrengths 34 Report. However, that does not mean I do not care. It means that I usually do not start my thinking or speaking from a place of empathy.

> Empathy and compassion are good bedfellows.

It just means that someone else's shoes do not fit me. How could they? I am not them. I do not have their set of circumstances, life experiences or life expectations. I can, however, listen and recognize what they may be feeling. I have been criticized for having low empathy and because I have openly shared this, it has colored others' views of me. Some people are surprised by this information because I actively exhibit care to those around me. I just do not see it as my responsibility to feel someone's else's feelings. Instead, I approach people with compassion, care and concern. I liken this to that of a shepherd caring for her flock. The good news in having low empathy is that I can often leave the burdens of the day at the office and do not often suffer from empathy fatigue. Sometimes it's easier for leaders to have lower empathy in order to better manage the volume of emotions expressed around them on a daily basis. You want to be a leader that is making thoughtful, fact-based decisions, not decisions on an emotional whim.

On the flip side of this coin, you may be a leader who has high empathy. If you easily absorb and process the emotions of others from the day, it may be hard to leave it at the office. You have to be careful that your empathy is not overdone and leads to apathy instead. Managing emotions is very tiring work. You may need to step away from situations more often to avoid taking on the emotional weight of others so you can make decisions that in the best interest of your staff or department.

I submit to you for consideration that you employ compassion over empathy. According to *Greater Good Magazine*, compassion is defined as "the feeling that arises when you are confronted with another's suffering and feel motivated to relieve that suffering."[22]

While cynics may dismiss compassion as touchy-feely or irrational, scientists have started to map the biological basis of compassion, suggesting its deep evolutionary purpose. This research has shown that when we feel compassion, our heart rate slows down, we secrete the "bonding hormone" oxytocin, and regions of the brain linked to empathy, caregiving, and feelings of pleasure light up, which often results in our wanting to approach and care for other people.[22]

Now imagine you are a train conductor. You're sitting in the conductor's chair in the engine car. What is the role of the engine? The engine drives the train, right? Now imagine each car of the train holds different things. One car holds emotions, one car holds perceptions, one car holds the truth, and one car holds the past, or workplace expectations. Which car is your engine car? If we know emotions can make bad leaders, then we know that emotions cannot be the engine. While workplace expectations can change, the past does not; but is the past really at hand in the present moment? Probably not. The engine is the truth of the situation. It does not matter what the perceptions are if you have the truth and your goal is to keep the truth at the forefront.

I had a staff member who was regularly late for work. The traffic in our area is horrendous and I often find myself arriving later than I'd like regardless of how early I leave each morning for the office, so I get it. However, for this staff member, five minutes became ten minutes and then it became a half hour, then 40 minutes sometimes, which now started impacting other people in the office who had to pick up the slack when she was late. Our customers were also impacted. This staff member was also often quick to be the person to head out the door right at 5:00 p.m. I extended grace as long as a I could, but I finally had to put an end to this behavior. I scheduled a meeting to address the consistent tardiness. The employee did not believe that the tardiness was as persistent as I was describing. I presented her an excel spreadsheet documenting each tardy arrival during the previous three-week period. This was the truth and had nothing to do with my feelings about the employee. This is an example of the engine leading the train. It did not matter how I felt about the situation or the employee at this point. I had to present the facts (the truth) in this situation and offer a course correction.

Giving Feedback

In order to manage expectations and emotions, teaching your team how to address conflict and interpersonal communication can go a long way. Sometimes it is necessary and appropriate for you as the leader to address certain issues, especially if it is destructive to the team, the office culture, or violates an HR policy. However, if your team is not equipped to address conflict and give feedback, then they will either expect you to do it for them or it will come out in passive aggressive, or perhaps even aggressive ways. For better or worse, all of us learn how to do both of these things from our family of origin. Those skills or lack thereof not only impact our personal lives, but also overflow into the workplace. A method that I learned about recently at a workshop was called T.H.I.N.K.[23] This can be used in any situation in which feedback is necessary. Our entire staff has been trained to T.H.I.N.K. first so that everyone has the skills to give feedback to someone and positions the giver personal ownership of the message by using specific "I" statements.

Now when situations come up that may be a point of contention or create conflict, everyone is expected to walk through this model.

If they cannot answer 'yes' to all of these items, then it is likely a matter of perception or some other ill-intentioned communication. This may be employed in a situation in which the recipient may not be expecting or requesting it. It may also be to share something you appreciate about the person or share a behavior you noticed.

T- Is it True? Our perceptions are not facts. Consider your purpose and motive.
H - Is it Helpful? Is there an action item involved that the recipient can do differently?
I - Is it Inspirational? Look towards the future. The past cannot be changed.
N - is it necessary? Consider if this is important in the bigger picture.
K - is it kind? Your words should be respectful, void of sarcasm or negativity.

Another methodology that is similar to T.H.I.N.K that I learned about many years ago is called S.B.I.: Situation, Behavior, Impact. This feedback method allows the sender to give behavior-based information and take ownership for how it impacted them. This allows the message to be better received than if you use harsh words or point fingers.

For example, you could say:

"It really pissed me off that you did not help clean up the office after our event today. I don't understand why you shirk your responsibilities!"

How do you think this message may be received? Probably not very well.

Instead, use the S.B.I. method:

Situation: After our office event today. Behavior: You left the room and did not help me clean up. Impact: And that meant that I had to stay late to clean up, so I was late getting to an after-work appointment.

How do you think this message was received? Probably better than the first for sure. Certainly, the sender's approach, attitude and word choice can escalate or deescalate any situation in which feedback is offered.

People Are Who They Are

I will make note here, you do not want to wait too long to talk to someone when something happens. I think the general rule is that you must have any necessary conversation within three days of a situation. If you don't address it in a timely manner, that is on you, and you have to swallow it. You cannot be mad at another person or hold something against them because you did not have the courage to say something. If you wait too long and then decide a week later to say something, it is likely not going to land well no matter how you phrase it. I definitely have failed to give feedback in a timely manner on occasion and I just had to put it to rest. Remember what Andy Stanley said, "What you resist will persist." If you know you need to have a conversation with someone, the longer you avoid it, the more opportunities to have it will likely present itself. It is painful for you and unfair to the other person, who for all intents and purposes has no idea you're even upset or bothered by something they did.

Remember, you should always ask permission to provide feedback before you speak with a person. It could be a drop-by-their-office situation or it might be something you need to schedule because of your full calendars and the nature of the conversation. These types of conversations should also always be held in private and remain confidential between the two people involved.

At the end of the day, sometimes people cannot muster up the courage to give feedback to others, but it is your responsibility to teach them how to do it. Everyone has a record playing on repeat in their head that plays the songs of their life. They also have lives happening before, during and after the work hours that impact them. Sometimes people just have bad days and may or may not be able to manage their emotions. By having tough conversations and providing feedback, you are actually showing them compassion and giving them grace.

"There is nobility in compassion, a beauty in empathy, a grace in forgiveness." – John Connolly

STRATEGY TIME:

1. Learn and internalize the fact that how people treat other people is more a reflection of their relationship with themselves instead of with you (or colleagues). Then you'll be able to be more compassionate and extend grace where it is warranted.
2. Get to know your people, their lives, their worries, their personal goals and create opportunities in the workplace to sustain them.
3. You're only as successful as your least happy employee. Never underestimate them. They can wreak havoc on your team. You're not responsible for their happiness, but you are responsible for your team and you may need to have a difficult conversation with someone.
4. Never make an important decision based solely on how you feel about it. You must focus on the facts, the data, and the information available to you. Let the engine of truth drive your train. You can consider how the decision impacts others. As one of my former supervisors from early in my career, Von Stange, once said, "I'm here to make the best decision, not a popular one." Popular decisions are easy.

CHAPTER 12

Pretend They're Naked

"The truth is that fear is usually a comfort zone and mindset we have created for ourselves in order to avoid stepping out of our safety nets and confronting that which may make us feel uncomfortable." – Karlicia Lewis, author

Experience tells you what to do; confidence allows you to do it."
– Stan Smith, American former tennis player

Two of the biggest fears people have are burning to death and public speaking. One strategy you may be familiar with to help overcome the fear of public speaking is to pretend the audience is naked. When we're naked we are fully exposed and vulnerable. If you approach your leadership fears from the same place, it makes it a little less scary. Feel the fear and do it anyway. Acknowledging your fear is the first step into gaining confidence in your leadership. I remember the first time I got a job in which I would be one of the formal leaders of the office. I had been an internal candidate. The day I was offered and accepted the job, I left the office as a colleague and when I showed up the next morning, I was one of the bosses. I was terrified. But I took it one day at a time and with each small step, each new skill and every small success, I became more and more confident. You will have failures. And failure is a good teacher. Just don't get stuck in the failure. Instead learn from it. Just think of the many failures you have had thus far in life that have gotten you to your current position.

Remember, competence leads to confidence.

Leading well is hard and it is a scary prospect. There is so much to consider and keep in mind in any given moment and with each person under your care. It's a huge responsibility because the decisions you make even as a middle manager impacts the lives of others in big and small ways. This final chapter will offer you some final tips and tricks for your leadership toolkit, which will help build your confidence. Just remember what Les Brown says, "Everything that is hard isn't always worth it, but everything that is worth it, is always hard."

Extras for Your Toolkit:

- If you change your thinking, your feelings will eventually catch up and change too. Keep a feel-good file for the rough days. This may include thank you notes, emails or cards from the past. As Henry Ford said, "Whether you think you can, or you think you can't—you're right."
- Read! Resources in the form of books, periodicals and online resources. A quick Google search will give you countless articles.
- Talk to others who are better than you in areas you want to grow as a leader.
- When you ask a group a question soliciting a response, wait nine seconds. This gives the introverts in your group time to think about their response. Just ask your question and then count silently in your head to nine. It works every time.
- There is a time and a place for everything, but I have found if you ask questions to get your point across instead of stating

your point, it is better received. This takes some practice, but it will become second nature before you know it.
- Think about your motives and always do the right thing for the right reasons.

In Lysa Terkeurst's book, *It's Not Supposed to be This Way*, she talks about how we steer where we stare. She tells a story of how she was following a friend on the highway to a destination on an unfamiliar route. Traffic was heavy and cars were moving in between one another rapidly. Her friend's car got out of her sight, but she didn't realize it and continued to follow a car that looked exactly like her friend's. She ended up following that car into the driveway of a home where people she did not know lived. It is a really funny story and I found myself laughing out loud as I read it, but her illustration of how we as people steer where we stare is so true. If we're focused on our goals, we achieve them. If we get distracted by the latest shiny object, we start steering towards that and get off track. The same is true with leadership. When you are leading, you always have to steer your team toward the mission and vision of your department or office. You have to stay laser focused. This is hard to do because the environment where your department is housed may distract you and have you veer off in a new direction, and sometimes you have to run over there before you can come back to your own race.

A lot of leaders get bogged down with managerial tasks. Things like paperwork and reports are always wrestling for your time. You feel like you are always plugging the dam. I know I feel this way a lot, but leaders do what must be done. I have sat at the front desk answering the telephone and I've also cleaned out the full-sized refrigerator (which was gross by the way) in an effort to keep the boat afloat. It's OK. That's what leaders do. Helping your team in times of craziness increases your moral authority. There is no job that the leader should not be willing or able to do. Plus, most crazy seasons do not last forever. After completing these tasks though, remember to steer back to why you are there and lead your team.

Becoming a good leader is energizing and when all cylinders are firing, it is exhilarating. It can also be tiring. Trying to keep all of the balls in the air can be daunting and at times overwhelming. You may feel that you've been bonked around and bruised by the things that have happened to you and your confidence is shot. If that's you, find a way to take some time off and recharge. Do things that are meaningful to you. Spend time with people you care about. Get away for a long weekend to a place you've always wanted to visit. Get reacquainted with yourself. You'll remember who you are and why you are doing good work. Rely on the experiences you have had and come back refreshed with some new ideas.

You may be thinking, "There's so much I don't know." While that may be true, you have to start somewhere. What do you want to know? How do you want to grow? You don't know what you don't know and that's OK. Reading this book is a great start. Hopefully, your wheels are spinning, and you've taken some notes, dog-eared a few pages, or highlighted a thing or two. Attend a leadership conference. Watch Ted Talks. Find a leadership podcast. Find a leader in your organization and invite them to lunch or a coffee and pick their brain. Whatever you decide, set goals and start small.

Stepping into a middle management position can leave anyone shaking in their shoes. The word fear is both a noun and a verb. It is an emotion and an action. But it lives in our thinking. Real or imagined it can stop you in your tracks, but even when you are afraid and do not feel confident, act like you are. Eventually your feelings will catch up to your actions. You can start with low stakes efforts. And remember, you don't have to do everything all at once. Pick one of the quotes below to put on the bathroom mirror or somewhere in your office. They are good reminders about mindset.

> *"F.E.A.R. has two meanings — Forget Everything and Run or Face Everything and Rise. The choice is yours."*
> *– Zig Ziglar, author, salesman and motivational speaker*

> *"Thinking will not overcome fear, but action will."*
> *– W. Clement Stone, businessman and author of*
> <u>Believe and Achieve</u>

Pretend They're Naked

"Do the thing you fear to do and keep on doing it...that is the quickest and surest way ever yet discovered to conquer fear."
– Dale Carnegie

STRATEGY TIME

1. Do it afraid.
2. Keep your communication with your team high. This will keep chaos low.
3. Get over yourself. As Ken Coleman says in *The Proximity Principle*, there are two limiting beliefs that hold us back: Pride and Fear. Which one is limiting you?
4. Have a servant's attitude. Don't let your pride get in the way.
5. Be the person you want to work with. Model the way.
6. Never stop learning. Growth as a leader is not a quick fix proposition...it's a journey of trial and error, failure and success.
7. Select someone you like, and you already trust or are willing to develop a trust-based relationship to mentor you. This is someone who will give you feedback to help you grow. Someone you can bounce ideas off of. Someone you can vent to when you've had a rough day.
8. Find like-minded leaders to meet with regularly over coffee or lunch, in person or Zoom to share ideas, concerns and seek feedback.
9. "Don't Stop Until You're Proud" - Unknown

About the Author

Karen was born in North Carolina where she lived until she was 11, when her family moved to Virginia. Growing up, she was a leader in a variety of school and church-based groups, and it was in these environments that her leadership journey began. During the summers between junior and senior year in high school, Karen took part in a foreign exchange student program the German-American Partnership and lived with a different family each summer in Heidenheim, Germany.

Karen graduated from Radford University, located in southwest Virginia, with a Bachelor of Arts and continued her studies at Appalachian State University, located in Boone, North Carolina, miles from the Blue Ridge Parkway, where she earned a Master of Arts degree. During her undergraduate experience, Karen continued to lead on campus, serving as a New Student Orientation leader for two summers and a Resident Assistant for two years before becoming a hall director (aka "dorm mother") her senior year, a position typically held by a graduate student. While at Appalachian State, Karen held a graduate assistantship as a hall director, leading a team of undergraduate Resident Assistants and overseeing a 7-story residence hall filled with first-year college students.

Since that time, Karen has worked for the University of Tennessee-Knoxville, Webster College, University of South Dakota,

University of North Carolina-Chapel Hill, North Carolina State University and College of Charleston in a variety of roles and capacities. Each position came with its own set of leadership challenges and areas of growth and with each one, Karen assumed greater levels of responsibility, authority, and supervision, all within systems that were very well-established. In between Tennessee and South Dakota, Karen was an AmeriCorps participant for a year, serving as a Volunteer Coordinator for Indian River County in Vero Beach, Florida. Most recently, Karen completed her two-year term as a Region Chair for her professional organization. Prior to embracing that role, Karen chaired a Regional conference, alongside a dedicated team of colleagues, hosting 300 people for two days. Each new location and experience taught Karen valuable leadership lessons. Some have been transformative. Some have been painful. But all have been valuable.

Throughout her professional life, Karen has been a voracious consumer of leadership training opportunities by reading books and attending seminars, webinars, workshops, and conferences. These experiences have also led her to train in other areas of interest as well. As a result, Karen is a certified Myers-Briggs Type Indicator (Step I and II) facilitator, a certified Appreciation at Work facilitator, a StrengthsFinder® Coach and most recently joined the faculty for the NACADA Administrator's Institute. She has authored two articles in *Academic Advising Today* and co-authored an article in the *Metropolitan University Journal*. She has also facilitated over 25 professional presentations on topics such as collaboration, learning communities, generational diversity, needs assessment, workplace appreciation, and student spirituality.

Karen's passion is to continue to grow as a leader herself and have others benefit from the wisdom she has gained from her own experiences, so they can grow and develop as leaders themselves. Everyone that has a job spends more waking hours there than they may spend at home or with their families. That workplace should be effective, functional, and fun for everyone, including the defined leader. Karen wants to equip anyone in a leadership role to be a great

About the Author

leader and thrive. Because if they do, then the people who work for them will thrive as well.

During her free time, Karen enjoys attending cultural and performing arts events, planting new and interesting plants in her garden, and hosting others in her home. She is also a year-round volunteer for Samaritan's Purse Operation Christmas Child ministry and is always on the lookout for a great find for a shoebox. Karen currently lives in Charleston, SC with her husband, Tom, and their teenage son. Their daughter graduated from Western Carolina University.

Karen can be reached at kbhauschild@gmail.com or at karenhauschild.com.

Acknowledgements

I have always wanted to write a book, but I wasn't sure what I wanted my first book to be about and certainly had no idea what it takes to become a published author. I have so many ideas and there is so much to say, but it wasn't until I was reading Ken Coleman's *Proximity Principle* that I became convinced that now was the time. He discusses limiting beliefs, the lies, that stand in our way in life: pride and fear. Just the day prior, I said to one of my best friends, "If I write a book, then someone will have to read it." Cold stone fear.

That very next day, I learned about the Ultimate 48-hour Author and Ultimate World Publishing team and the journey began. I believe finding them when I did was divinely inspired as was the subject I landed on and the title for this book. Thank you, Nat, Stu, Julie, Vivi and Nik. I have learned so much, not only about myself, but also about the world of publishing. I also thank my fellow authors from all over the world who are writing alongside me. Thank you for sharing yourselves with me. You are some fantastic folks.

To my home team, my husband Tom, and our children, Holly and Carson. And to Kalen, my son from another mother. Thank you for ready encouragement, serving as my biggest cheerleaders and feedback givers. Thank you all for supporting me every step of the way and telling everyone you know about the book. I have spent countless hours pouring over the content and every detail in these pages, and I pray it will bless every reader.

A special shout out to my daughter, Holly, who designed my logo. She is so creative. I could not have created anything so stunning.

To my best friends, Penney and Jennifer. Thank you for the gift of friendship. You, too, have been my greatest supporters along life's journey, including this newest adventure, and I am thankful. Penney, thank you for being my first editor and formal feedback giver and to Jennifer for being the person on the other end of the telephone when I decided it was time to write this book.

To the women in my small group Bible study: Jerri, Giovonni, Janet, Tara and Brenda. Thank you for your encouragement to go for it, as well as your prayer and support all along the way.

To my home away from home team, my work team at the Academic Advising and Planning Center (AAPC) at the College of Charleston, both past and present. I have learned so much from each and every one of you. Thank you for the privilege to lead you. I do my best to lead well every day because of you. A special shout out to my current team members in the AAPC: Anne, Bill, Brian, Emily, Hayden, John, Julie, Kari, Katie, Lauren, Leona, Raymond, Silvia and Tradd. Thank you also to my fellow directors in the Academic Experience and my friends and colleagues in other departments and across the country. I have appreciated the lunches, coffee talks, zoom chats and phone calls as we navigate the world of middle management together.

Thank you to the great supervisors I have worked with in my career, in particular, Dr. Lynne Ford, Dr. Carrie McLean and Sandy Curtis. I have learned countless lessons from your leadership and it has been a privilege to work with you.

And thank you to all the authors, many of whom I have referenced in this book, whom I only know through their words. Your thoughts and ideas have connected with my own and have helped shape my own development as a leader. I hope we meet someday in person.

Afterward

To be sure, growing as a leader is a work in progress, and I am no exception. Every day I try to make fewer mistakes than I did the day before. You just have to keep learning and keep trying. I hope the contents of this book encourages you and gives you some practical strategies and new ideas that you can employ right away. In my experience, I have found that very few organizations care about people. People care about people. May you lead well.

Karen Hauschild

is an experienced presenter, workshop facilitator, consultant, and a trained educator with a unique 30-year career in higher education. She has a background in leadership and communication, organization and planning achieving industry leading results.

Karen believes that good leadership comes from never giving up and always trying to better yourself. It also comes from giving yourself a break—you can't do it right every time; but even if you're aiming for the bullseye, you must take the blindfold off. A better you, makes a better leader.

Karen is an engaging, interactive, approachable speaker and facilitator who offers practical can-do strategies to thrive in the leadership trenches by telling stories and sharing real-life examples to inspire you to become a better leader.

Karen has a bachelor's degree in speech communication and a master's degree in Student Development alongside decades of experience as a middle manager, winning numerous awards, recognition and accolades. She is certified in both the Myers-Briggs Type Indicator and as an Appreciation in the Workplace facilitator. She has also been trained in Gallop's Clifton Strengths.

KAREN HAUSCHILD

Contact Karen to discuss your event tailored to your needs:

Thriving as a Leader
- Identifying Your Values and Employing Them to Your Benefit
- Appreciative Leadership
- Resource Utilization and Making Something from Nothing

Resetting Your Workplace Culture
- Assessing Your Team's Culture
- How to Take Your Staff from Toxic to Take-Off
- Implementing Agreed Upon Values

Finding and Retaining Great Employees
- Understanding Why People Leave
- Key Strategies to Developing a Solid Process
- How to Teach Your Team Values, Competencies and Skills

Contact Karen to speak at your next event or facilitate your team's next retreat or workshop.

✉ kbhauschild@gmail.com 📞 919-302-6573

Offers

Meet Me In the Trenches:
Do you feel like you need to take the first steps in unearthing what you need to work on or where you should begin in your leadership?

Free Offer: One 20-minute consultation to address your burning question or concern. Valued at $50.

Contact Karen at kbhauschild@gmail.com to schedule.

Filling in the Trench:
Begin the process of laying a foundation with solid team building and establishing ground level trust through a two-hour to four-hour workshop for your staff. What does your team need? What do you need to assess? Customized to meet your needs.

Contact Karen at kbhauschild@gmail.com for pricing and to schedule.

Major Construction:
Perhaps your team is already on solid ground and you would like to take it to the to next level by having them complete and process

a personal assessment. Or you have made your plans, but now you need to work the plan. Perhaps you have a problem to solve that must involve your team to arrive at the solution. Better equip your team to achieve personal and professional goals or solve a problem facing your department or company through a half-day, full-day or multi-day workshop that is fully customized to meet your goals and objectives.

Contact Karen at kbhauschild@gmail.com for pricing and to schedule.

Testimonials

"Whether it's leading in her workplace, facilitating a workshop, or presenting at professional development conferences, Karen Hauschild understands how to lead with excellence. In her words and actions, she facilitates cooperation through mutual respect, creativity, and commitment to continuing growth. An inspirational mentor and excellent communicator, she knows how to convey a vision, plan detailed strategies, coordinate collaborative teams, and achieve goals, all with a heart that values the individual within the systems she creates."

Carol B. Wilson
Professor of English
Wofford College

"Karen is an authentic, action-oriented leader who can motivate teams to maximum functionality. She is an engaging and dynamic facilitator who keeps an eye to progressive team goal development and attainment."

Dr. Carrie F. McLean

References

Chapter 1: Only the Lonely
1. Apollo Technical Engineered Talent Solutions. (2021, December 19). *25 Surprising Leadership Statistics..* https://www.apollotechnical.com/leadership-statistics/

Lencioni, Patrick. *The Motive*. Wiley: 2020.

Chapter 2: Captain of My Ship
2. Stanley, Andy, Leadership Podcast, Visioneering Part 2, November 4, 2016.

   Downer, Ken. *Leaders Go First: The Surprising Impact of Making the First Move*. Rapid Start Leadership. https://www.rapidstartleadership.com/leaders-go-first/*Mt Everest*

3. Leger, C.J. (2016, December 31). *The 1996 Everest Disaster- The Whole Story*. Base Camp Magazine. https://basecampmagazine.com/2016/12/31/the-1996-everest-disaster-the-whole-story/

Titanic
4. Daugherty, Greg. *What Was the Titanic's Captain Doing While the Ship Sank?* History. Com. https://www.history.com/news/titanic-captain-edward-smith-final-hours-death

Cruise Ship
5. (2015, February 11). *Costa Concordia Captain Schettino Guilty of Manslaughter.* BBC News. https://www.bbc.com/news/world-europe-31430998

Leadership Styles:
6. Indeed Editorial Team. (2021, December 8). *10 Common Leadership Styles (Plus How to Find Your Own).* Indeed. https://www.indeed.com/career-advice/career-development/10-common-leadership-styles

7. Kenton, Will. (2020, September 28). *What is the Hersey-Blanchard Model?* Investopedia. https://www.investopedia.com/terms/h/hersey-and-blanchard-model.asp

Chapter 3: The Middle Child
Elliot, Brian. (2021, May 21). *It's Time to Free the Middle Manager.* Harvard Business Review. https://hbr.org/2021/05/its-time-to-free-the-middle-manager (opening quote)

Chapter 4: Man in the Mirror
8. MBTI
   https://www.myersbriggs.org/my-mbti-personality-type/mbti-basics/the-16-mbti-types.htm
   https://www.myersbriggs.org/my-mbti-personality-type/take-the-mbti-instrument/

9. Clifton Strengths/Clifton StrengthsFinder
   https://www.gallup.com/cliftonstrengths/en/252137/home.aspx
   https://www.gallup.com/cliftonstrengths/en/253868/popular-cliftonstrengths-assessment-products.aspx

10. Stand Out
    https://www.marcusbuckingham.com/gift-of-standout/

11. DiSC
    https://www.discprofile.com/what-is-disc/disc-styles
    https://www.discprofile.com/
    https://discpersonalitytesting.com/

References

Bud To Boss
https://www.budtoboss.com/

12. Keirsey Temperament Sorter
https://keirsey.com/

13. Baker, Mary, contact. (2019, October 29). *Gartner Says Only 13% of Employees are Largely Satisfied With Their Work Experiences*. Gartner Newsroom Press Release. https://www.gartner.com/en/newsroom/press-releases/2019-10-29-gartner-says-only-13--of-employees-are-largely-satisf

Chapter 5: A Matter of Taste
Sare, John, 2020, Values Survey Pre/Post Survey.

Chapter 6: Needle in a Haystack

14. Boskamp, Elsie. (2022, January 5). *Average Cost Per Hire [2022]: All Cost of Hiring Statistics*. Zippia: The Career Expert. https://www.zippia.com/advice/cost-of-hiring-statistics-average-cost-per-hire/

15. 5. Lazic, Marja, (2021, February 10) *30 Mind-Blowing Interview Statistics to Get You Going in 2021*. https://legaljobs.io/blog/interview-statistics/#:~:text=The%20average%20number%20of%20interviews,ll%20just%20fi nd%20new%20candidates

Lencioni, Patrick. *The Ideal Team Player*. Jossey-Bass: 2016.

Chapter 7: Do Not Pass Go
16. Tuckman's Stages of Group Development

West Chester University. Collaborative On-Line Research and Learning. *Tuckman's Stages of Group Development* https://www.wcupa.edu/coral/tuckmanStagesGroupDelvelopment.aspx#:~:text=These%20stages%20are%20commonly%20known,more%20collaborative%20or%20shared%20leadership)

Kumar, Pramod. (2020, August 28) *Tuckman's Stages of Group Development*. https://slidebazaar.com/blog/tuckmans-theory-of-team-development/

Wilson, Carol. Bruce Tuckman: Culture At Work. *The Forming, Storming, Norming and Performing Team Development Model*. https://www.coachingcultureatwork.com/bruce-tuckman-team-development-model/

Chapter 8: I Didn't Volunteer for This

17. Vuleta, Branka. (2021, February 1) *23+ Fascinating Job Satisfaction Stats [2022 Update]*. Legaljobs. https://legaljobs.io/blog/job-satisfaction-stats/

18. True Colors
https://www.truecolorsintl.com/what-is-true-colors

Chapter 9: I Did a Great Job, I Promise

19. Sutton, Robert and Wigert, Ben. (2019, May 6) *More Harm Than Good: The Truth About Performance Reviews*. Gallup.com. https://www.gallup.com/workplace/249332/harm-good-truth-performance-reviews.aspx

20. Lettink, Anita (2019, September 17) *No, Millenials will NOT be 75% of the Workforce in 2025 (or ever)!* Linkedin. https://www.linkedin.com/pulse/millenials-75-workforce-2025-ever-anita-lettink

Chapter 10: Multi…what?

Generational Diversity

21. Crossing the Generational Divide Workshop, April 2015, Carrie Messal, PhD., Associate Professor of Management and Marketing, College of Charleston School of Business.

    Trunk, Penelope. *(2007, October 17). The real deal about Gen Y: they're inherently conservative*. http://blog.penelopetrunk.com/2007/10/17/the-real-deal-about-gen-y-theyre-inherently-conservative/

    Trunk, Penelope (2011, March 30). *Generation Z will revolutionize education*, http://blog.penelopetrunk.com/2011/03/30/generation-z-will-revolutionize-education/

References

Trunk, Penelope (2012, Dec. 21) *How the next generation will surpass Gen Y*, http://blog.penelopetrunk.com/2012/12/21/why-the-next-generation-will-hate-gen-y/

Trunk, Penelope (2015, *March 24). What Leadership will look like when Generation Z takes over (and I hope Pope Francis).* http://blog.penelopetrunk.com/2015/03/24/what-leadership-will-look-like-when-generation-z-takes-over-and-i-love-pope-francis/

sparks & honey. (2014, June 17). *Meet Generation Z: Forget Everything You Learned about Millennials.* http://www.slideshare.net/sparksandhoney/generation-z-final-june-17/1

Patel, Deep. (2017, September 21). *8 Ways Generation Z Will Differ From Millennials in the Workplace.* https://www.forbes.com/sites/deeppatel/2017/09/21/8-ways-generation-z-will-differ-frommillennials-in-the-workplace/#1ce2c4ce76e5

The Kasasa Exchange. (2021, July 6). *Boomers, Gen X, Gen Y, Gen Z and Gen A explained.* https://www.kasasa.com/exchange/articles/generations/gen-x-gen-y-gen-z

Carter, Christine. (2016, December 21). *The Complete Guide to Generation Alpha, The Children of Millennials.* https://www.forbes.com/sites/christinecarter/2016/12/21/the-complete-guide-to-generation-alpha-the-children-of-millennials/?sh=6f9c67da3623

Chapter 11: Managing Emotions

22. Greater Good Magazine. *What is Compassion?* The Greater Good Science Center at the University of California, Berkeley. https://greatergood.berkeley.edu/topic/compassion/definition

23. Sheridan, Elayne, workshop facilitator. *Interpersonal Communication and Conflict Resolution Skills,* November 7, 2019.

Terkeurst, Lysa. *It's Not Supposed to be this Way.* Nelson Books: 2018.

Stanley, Andy. *The Principle of the Path.* Thomas Nelson: 2008.

Chapter 12: Pretend They're Naked
Lewise, Karlicia. *Four Truths about Fear We Tend to Overlook.* https://www.lifehack.org/523521/4-truths-about-fear-tend-overlook

Notes

Leadership in the Trenches

Notes

Leadership in the Trenches

Notes

www.ingramcontent.com/pod-product-compliance
Lightning Source LLC
Chambersburg PA
CBHW021148080526
44588CB00008B/258